Lord Macaulay

The Works of
Lord Macaulay

❧

*with an Introduction by Donald Hawes,
and Bibliography*

Wordsworth Poetry Library

This edition published 1995 by Wordsworth Editions Ltd,
Cumberland House, Crib Street, Ware, Hertfordshire SG12 9ET.

ISBN 1-85326-448-2

Typeset in the UK by Antony Gray.
Printed and bound in Denmark by Nørhaven.

INTRODUCTION

Thomas Babington Macaulay led a life of unceasing intellectual, political and administrative activity. He was born on 25 October 1800, the eldest son of Zachary and Selina Macaulay, who were prominent members of the so-called Clapham Sect, a group of Evangelical reformers and philanthropists who were in the forefront of the campaign for the abolition of slavery. From the time he was three years old, he was constantly absorbed in reading, often while lying in front of the fire with a piece of bread and butter in his hand. He astonished everyone with his feats of memory, his range of knowledge and his compositions in verse and prose. After leaving Trinity College, Cambridge, Macaulay rapidly made a reputation as a brilliant essayist on historical and literary topics, particularly in the *Edinburgh Review* from 1825 onwards. He entered the House of Commons as a Whig in 1830 and distinguished himself as a robust speaker, soon taking a notable part in the debates on the Reform Bill. From 1834 to 1838 he was in India, as a member of the Governor General's Supreme Council. He was influential there in establishing reformed educational and penal systems. On his return to England, he re-entered Parliament, twice holding Cabinet office, as Secretary at War and as Paymaster General in the administrations of Lord Melbourne and Lord John Russell. At the same time as carrying out his public duties, he continued his cherished activities of reading and authorship, producing essays replete with learning, eloquence and wit, poems, and – setting the seal on his reputation as an historian – his best-selling *History of England* (1848 and 1855). He was raised to the peerage in 1857. Macaulay, who had suffered from ill-health for several years, died on 28 December 1859 while seated in his library chair. He was buried in Westminster Abbey on 9 January 1860.

In his early years the first generation of the Romantic poets –

Wordsworth, Coleridge, Scott and Southey – were at the height of their creativity. Macaulay had little sympathy with sentimentality, the transcendental and the worship of Nature. What appealed to him was the colour and excitement of poems of adventure and heroism in historical or legendary times. His mother recounted that as an eight-year-old boy he was 'so fired with reading Scott's *Lay* [*of the Last Minstrel*] and *Marmion*, the former of which he got entirely, and the latter almost entirely, by heart, merely from his delight in reading them, that he determined on writing himself a poem in six cantos which he called the "Battle of Cheviot".' He always remembered the first thrilling impression made on him by Coleridge's *The Rime of the Ancient Mariner*, enjoyed Southey's *Thalaba* and *Curse of Kehama,* and at nineteen was writing lines in imitation of Byron. In addition, he memorised much of Shakespeare and all of *Paradise Lost*. As he testifies in his famous essay on Milton, that poet's 'muster-rolls of names' transport readers to distant ages and regions and fill the imagination with 'chivalrous romance'. He had a life-long fondness for English ballads old and new, buying (so his nephew, Sir G. O. Trevelyan, tells us in his biography) 'every half-penny song on which he could lay his hands; if only it was decent, and a genuine, undoubted poem of the people'. Macaulay was steeped in classical literature, which he seems to have read almost daily, and had an incomparable knowledge of ancient and modern history. For him, the great Greek and Roman historians – Herodotus, Thucydides, Livy and Tacitus – were supreme. His work as an essayist and later as the writer of the *History of England* involved him in intensive research, including the study of original documents and sometimes arduous fieldwork. When we consider his mastery of historical information combined with his appreciation of the metres and imagery of poets as different as the ballad-makers, Milton and Scott, we can begin to understand how and why Macaulay's poetry acquired its particular shape and material. It is learned and literary (but not pedantic or didactic) and at the same time it has the direct appeal of a ballad.

Its immediately striking features are its emphatic rhythms and its strong but seemingly inevitable rhymes. He always had an instinctive command of metre. 'He had no notion whatever of music,' Sir George Trevelyan states, 'but an infallible ear for rhythm.' When very young, he could write poetic 'epics' with ease, and throughout his life he possessed the gift of improvising precise and elegant verse on any occasion. The metrical patterns in his published poetry are inseparable from his typical themes of heroism, patriotism and conflict, since they convey speed and force to the ear, as in these heptameters from 'The Armada':

> And from the furthest wards was heard the
> rush of hurrying feet,
> And the broad streams of pikes and flags
> rushed down each roaring street;
> And broader still became the blaze, and louder
> still the din,
> As fast from every village round the horse came
> spurring in.

Along with his incantatory rhythms go his evocative lists of names and his splendid descriptions, like that of the 'painted hall' in 'The Marriage of Tirzah and Ahirad', where the dazzled spectator sees, among much else,

> The crystal founts whence sparkling flow
> The richest wines o'er beds of snow,
> The walls where blaze in living dyes
> The king's three hundred victories.

As the critic 'Christopher North' exclaimed in *Blackwood's Magazine* when the *Lays of Ancient Rome* were first published in 1842, 'Macaulay is full of fire.' The poems certainly appealed to his contemporaries, since (according to Trevelyan) 'by June 1875, upwards of a hundred thousand copies had passed into the hands of readers'. For a hundred years or so they could be recited, at least in part, by schoolboys (rather than schoolgirls). They remain admirable pieces to read aloud.

Macaulay started to write the *Lays* in India. He believed in a theory, proposed by a number of scholars, that the 'romantic tales [of the early history of Rome] which fill the first three or four books of Livy, came from the lost ballads of the early Romans'. He developed the theory and supplied extensive discussions of the background to the poems in a general Introduction and individual prefaces. He said that in the *Lays* 'the author speaks, not in his own person, but in the persons of ancient minstrels who know only what a Roman citizen, born three or four hundred years before the Christian era, may be supposed to have known, and who are in nowise above the passions and prejudices of their age and nation'. Both 'Horatius' and 'The Battle of the Lake Regillus' blend the history and legends, as found in Livy and other sources, of two of the three attempts by Tarquin to recover the throne of Rome. Macaulay would have expected his readers to understand his references to Roman personages and places, as he always overestimated other people's knowledge of literature, philosophy and history. After all, he wrote that often-quoted sentence in his essay on Clive: 'Every schoolboy knows who imprisoned Montezuma, and who strangled Atahualpa.' Most of his references will elude today's readers, who in any case lack the grounding in the classics many of Macaulay's readers would have had, but the sweeping eloquence of his metrical narratives of heroism, victory and defeat is irresistible. That eloquence cannot be dismissed as empty rhetoric, as Macaulay time after time achieves effects of dramatic concision.

> And even the ranks of Tuscany
> Could scarce forbear to cheer

from 'Horatius' has become proverbial because of its memorable encapsulation of a particular idea, but many similar striking expressions can be found, as in his precise description of the fall of the bridge:

> But with a crash like thunder
> Fell every loosened beam,
> And, like a dam, the mighty wreck
> Lay right athwart the stream:
> And a long shout of triumph
> Rose from the walls of Rome,
> As to the highest turret-tops
> Was splashed the yellow foam.

In 'The Battle of the Lake Regillus' (in which Herminius, one of the three who 'kept the bridge', reappears), Macaulay makes exciting use of his observation in his preface that the battle 'is in all respects a Homeric battle, except that the combatants ride astride their horses, instead of driving chariots' and that 'the leaders single each other out, and engage hand to hand'. The two horses, 'black Auster' and 'the dark-grey charger', become heroic characters in their own right. An eerie poetic realisation of his source material is his picture of the apparition of Castor and Pollux, who have come to help the Romans:

> White as snow their armour was:
> Their steeds were white as snow.

'Virginia', with its account of a young girl killed by her father to save her from 'servitude and dishonour' (to use Macaulay's phrase), celebrates the defiance of tyranny. 'The Prophecy of Capys' foretells the glories that will be associated with the 'mighty name of Rome'.

'The Marriage of Tirzah and Ahirad', a superb declamatory poem that is little known today, sensuously evokes the 'festal mirth' and 'pomp' at the wedding of the brave son of Seth to the loveliest woman of 'all the house of Cain'. Jubal's 'lofty song' is followed by the prophecy of the Flood, both expressed with inventive exuberance. Macaulay, who always upheld the principles of Protestantism and the Glorious Revolution of 1688, as is clear in his essays and *History of England* and indeed in his political life, glories in the defeat of the Spanish Armada by the English fleet in 1588, in King Henry IV's victory over the Catholic League at Ivry in 1590 and in Cromwell's rout of the Royalist army at Naseby in 1645. But his 'Epitaph on a Jacobite' is a moving tribute to the 'courage and faith' of a Royalist, expressed in subtly varied rhyming couplets.

The assertiveness and confidence of his tone and subject matter markedly contrast with the diffidence, introspection and ironies that are valued as poetic qualities by many critics. Admitting that Macaulay's poetry lacked exquisiteness and variety of poetic thought, George Saintsbury in his *Short History of English Literature* (1898) was nevertheless forthright in his advocacy of its popular appeal: 'Those who do not recognise the poetic quality in it show that their poetical thermometer is deficient in delicacy and range.' If today we read it without prejudice, we are sure to respond delightedly to Macaulay's masterly technique, his bravura, and his evident joy in communicating to his readers his excitement about historical and legendary heroes and deeds.

Donald Hawes
University of Westminster and
The Open University

FURTHER READING

Sir G. O. Trevelyan, *The Life and Letters of Lord Macaulay*, 1876, enlarged, 1908

Sir Arthur Bryant, *Macaulay*, 1932

Jane Millgate, *Macaulay*, 1973

John Clive, *Thomas Babington Macaulay: The Shaping of the Historian*, 1974

Kenneth Young, *Macaulay*, 1976

Thomas Pinney (ed.), *The Selected Letters of Thomas Babington Macaulay*, 1982

Owen Dudley Edwards, *Macaulay*, 1988

CONTENTS

LAYS OF ANCIENT ROME

Horatius

**A LAY MADE ABOUT
THE YEAR OF THE CITY
CCCLX**

1

Lars Porsena of Clusium
  By the Nine Gods he swore
That the great house of Tarquin
  Should suffer wrong no more.
By the Nine Gods he swore it,
  And named a trysting day,
And bade his messengers ride forth,
East and west and south and north,
  To summon his array.

2

East and west and south and north
  The messengers ride fast,
And tower and town and cottage
  Have heard the trumpet's blast.
Shame on the false Etruscan
  Who lingers in his home,
When Porsena of Clusium
  Is on the march for Rome.

3

The horsemen and the footmen
  Are pouring in amain
From many a stately market-place;
  From many a fruitful plain;
From many a lonely hamlet,
  Which, hid by beech and pine,
Like an eagle's nest, hangs on the crest
  Of purple Apennine;

4

From lordly Volaterræ,
    Where scowls the far-famed hold
Piled by the hands of giants
    For godlike kings of old;
From seagirt Populonia,
    Whose sentinels descry
Sardinia's snowy mountain-tops
    Fringing the southern sky;

5

From the proud mart of Pisæ,
    Queen of the western waves,
Where ride Massilia's triremes
    Heavy with fair-haired slaves;
From where sweet Clanis wanders
    Through corn and vines and flowers;
From where Cortona lifts to heaven
    Her diadem of towers.

6

Tall are the oaks whose acorns
    Drop in dark Auser's rill;
Fat are the stags that champ the boughs
    Of the Ciminian hill;
Beyond all streams Clitumnus
    Is to the herdsman dear;
Best of all pools the fowler loves
    The great Volsinian mere.

7

But now no stroke of woodman
    Is heard by Auser's rill;
No hunter tracks the stag's green path
    Up the Ciminian hill;

Unwatched along Clitumnus
   Grazes the milk-white steer;
Unharmed the water fowl may dip
   In the Volsinian mere.

8

The harvests of Arretium,
   This year, old men shall reap;
This year, young boys in Umbro
   Shall plunge the struggling sheep;
And in the vats of Luna,
   This year, the must shall foam
Round the white feet of laughing girls
   Whose sires have marched to Rome.

9

There be thirty chosen prophets,
   The wisest of the land,
Who alway by Lars Porsena
   Both morn and evening stand:
Evening and morn the Thirty
   Have turned the verses o'er,
Traced from the right on linen white
   By mighty seers of yore.

10

And with one voice the Thirty
   Have their glad answer given:
'Go forth, go forth, Lars Porsena;
   Go forth, beloved of Heaven;
Go, and return in glory
   To Clusium's royal dome;
And hang round Nurscia's altars
   The golden shields of Rome.'

11

And now hath every city
  Sent up her tale of men;
The foot are fourscore thousand,
  The horse are thousands ten.
Before the gates of Sutrium
  Is met the great array.
A proud man was Lars Porsena
  Upon the trysting day.

12

For all the Etruscan armies
  Were ranged beneath his eye,
And many a banished Roman,
  And many a stout ally;
And with a mighty following
  To join the muster came
The Tusculan Mamilius,
  Prince of the Latian name.

13

But by the yellow Tiber
  Was tumult and affright:
From all the spacious champaign
  To Rome men took their flight.
A mile around the city,
  The throng stopped up the ways;
A fearful sight it was to see
  Through two long nights and days.

14

For aged folk on crutches,
  And women great with child,
And mothers sobbing over babes
  That clung to them and smiled,

And sick men borne in litters
   High on the necks of slaves,
And troops of sun-burned husbandmen
   With reaping-hooks and staves,

15

And droves of mules and asses
   Laden with skins of wine,
And endless flocks of goats and sheep,
   And endless herds of kine,
And endless trains of waggons
   That creaked beneath the weight
Of corn-sacks and of household goods,
   Choked every roaring gate.

16

Now, from the rock Tarpeian,
   Could the wan burghers spy
The line of blazing villages
   Red in the midnight sky.
The Fathers of the City,
   They sat all night and day,
For every hour some horseman came
   With tidings of dismay.

17

To eastward and to westward
   Have spread the Tuscan bands;
Nor house, nor fence, nor dovecote
   In Crustumerium stands.
Verbenna down to Ostia
   Hath wasted all the plain;
Astur hath stormed Janiculum,
   And the stout guards are slain.

18

I wis, in all the Senate,
  There was no heart so bold,
But sore it ached, and fast it beat,
  When that ill news was told.
Forthwith up rose the Consul,
  Up rose the Fathers all;
In haste they girded up their gowns,
  And hied them to the wall.

19

They held a council standing,
  Before the River-Gate;
Short time was there, ye well may guess,
  For musing or debate.
Out spake the Consul roundly:
  'The bridge must straight go down;
For, since Janiculum is lost,
  Nought else can save the town.'

20

Just then a scout came flying,
  All wild with haste and fear:
'To arms! to arms! Sir Consul:
  Lars Porsena is here.'
On the low hills to westward
  The Consul fixed his eye,
And saw the swarthy storm of dust
  Rise fast along the sky.

21

And nearer fast and nearer
  Doth the red whirlwind come;
And louder still and still more loud,
From underneath that rolling cloud,
Is heard the trumpet's war-note proud,
  The trampling, and the hum.

And plainly and more plainly
  Now through the gloom appears,
Far to left and far to right,
In broken gleams of dark-blue light,
The long array of helmets bright,
  The long array of spears.

22

And plainly and more plainly,
  Above that glimmering line,
Now might ye see the banners
  Of twelve fair cities shine;
But the banner of proud Clusium
  Was highest of them all,
The terror of the Umbrian,
  The terror of the Gaul.

23

And plainly and more plainly
  Now might the burghers know,
By port and vest, by horse and crest,
  Each warlike Lucumo.
There Cilnius of Arretium
  On his fleet roan was seen;
And Astur of the four-fold shield,
Girt with the brand none else may wield,
Tolumnius with the belt of gold,
And dark Verbenna from the hold
  By reedy Thrasymene.

24

Fast by the royal standard,
  O'erlooking all the war,
Lars Porsena of Clusium
  Sat in his ivory car.

By the right wheel rode Mamilius,
   Prince of the Latian name;
And by the left false Sextus,
   That wrought the deed of shame.

25

But when the face of Sextus
   Was seen among the foes,
A yell that rent the firmament
   From all the town arose.
On the house-tops was no woman
   But spat towards him and hissed,
No child but screamed out curses,
   And shook its little fist.

26

But the Consul's brow was sad,
   And the Consul's speech was low,
And darkly looked he at the wall,
   And darkly at the foe.
'Their van will be upon us
   Before the bridge goes down;
And if they once may win the bridge,
   What hope to save the town?'

27

Then out spake brave Horatius,
   The Captain of the gate:
'To every man upon this earth
   Death cometh soon or late.
And how can man die better
   Than facing fearful odds,
For the ashes of his fathers,
   And the temples of his Gods,

28

'And for the tender mother
  Who dandled him to rest,
And for the wife who nurses
  His baby at her breast,
And for the holy maidens
  Who feed the eternal flame,
To save them from false Sextus
  That wrought the deed of shame?

29

'Hew down the bridge, Sir Consul,
  With all the speed ye may;
I, with two more to help me,
  Will hold the foe in play.
In yon strait path a thousand
  May well be stopped by three.
Now who will stand on either hand,
  And keep the bridge with me?'

30

Then out spake Spurius Lartius;
  A Ramnian proud was he:
'Lo, I will stand at thy right hand,
  And keep the bridge with thee.'
And out spake strong Herminius;
  Of Titian blood was he:
'I will abide on thy left side,
  And keep the bridge with thee.'

31

'Horatius,' quoth the Consul,
  'As thou sayest, so let it be.'
And straight against that great array
  Forth went the dauntless Three.

For Romans in Rome's quarrel
   Spared neither land nor gold,
Nor son nor wife, nor limb nor life,
   In the brave days of old.

32

Then none was for a party;
   Then all were for the state;
Then the great man helped the poor,
   And the poor man loved the great:
Then lands were fairly portioned;
   Then spoils were fairly sold:
The Romans were like brothers
   In the brave days of old.

33

Now Roman is to Roman
   More hateful than a foe,
And the Tribunes beard the high,
   And the Fathers grind the low.
As we wax hot in faction,
   In battle we wax cold:
Wherefore men fight not as they fought
   In the brave days of old.

34

Now while the Three were tightening
   Their harness on their backs,
The Consul was the foremost man
   To take in hand an axe:
And Fathers mixed with Commons
   Seized hatchet, bar, and crow,
And smote upon the planks above,
   And loosed the props below.

35

Meanwhile the Tuscan army,
   Right glorious to behold,
Came flashing back the noonday light,
Rank behind rank, like surges bright
   Of a broad sea of gold.
Four hundred trumpets sounded
   A peal of warlike glee,
As that great host, with measured tread,
And spears advanced, and ensigns spread,
Rolled slowly towards the bridge's head,
   Where stood the dauntless Three.

36

The Three stood calm and silent,
   And looked upon the foes,
And a great shout of laughter
   From all the vanguard rose:
And forth three chiefs came spurring
   Before that deep array;
To earth they sprang, their swords they drew,
And lifted high their shields, and flew
   To win the narrow way;

37

Aunus from green Tifernum,
   Lord of the Hill of Vines;
And Seius, whose eight hundred slaves
   Sicken in Ilva's mines;
And Picus, long to Clusium
   Vassal in peace and war,
Who led to fight his Umbrian powers
From that grey crag where, girt with towers,
The fortress of Nequinum lowers
   O'er the pale waves of Nar.

38

Stout Lartius hurled down Aunus
   Into the stream beneath:
Herminius struck at Seius,
   And clove him to the teeth:
At Picus brave Horatius
   Darted one fiery thrust;
And the proud Umbrian's gilded arms
   Clashed in the bloody dust.

39

Then Ocnus of Falerii
   Rushed on the Roman Three;
And Lausulus of Urgo,
   The rover of the sea;
And Aruns of Volsinium,
   Who slew the great wild boar,
The great wild boar that had his den
Amidst the reeds of Cosa's fen,
And wasted fields, and slaughtered men,
   Along Albinia's shore.

40

Herminius smote down Aruns:
   Lartius laid Ocnus low:
Right to the heart of Lausulus
   Horatius sent a blow.
'Lie there,' he cried, 'fell pirate!
   No more, aghast and pale,
From Ostia's walls the crowd shall mark
The track of thy destroying bark.
No more Campania's hinds shall fly
To woods and caverns when they spy
   Thy thrice accursed sail.'

41

But now no sound of laughter
   Was heard amongst the foes.
A wild and wrathful clamour
   From all the vanguard rose.
Six spears' lengths from the entrance
   Halted that deep array,
And for a space no man came forth
   To win the narrow way.

42

But hark! the cry is Astur:
   And lo! the ranks divide;
And the great Lord of Luna
   Comes with his stately stride.
Upon his ample shoulders
   Clangs loud the four-fold shield,
And in his hand he shakes the brand
   Which none but he can wield.

43

He smiled on those bold Romans
   A smile serene and high;
He eyed the flinching Tuscans,
   And scorn was in his eye.
Quoth he, 'The she-wolf's litter
   Stand savagely at bay:
But will ye dare to follow,
   If Astur clears the way?'

44

Then, whirling up his broadsword
   With both hands to the height,
He rushed against Horatius,
   And smote with all his might.

With shield and blade Horatius
   Right deftly turned the blow.
The blow, though turned, came yet too nigh;
It missed his helm, but gashed his thigh:
The Tuscans raised a joyful cry
   To see the red blood flow.

45

He reeled, and on Herminius
   He leaned one breathing-space;
Then, like a wild cat mad with wounds
   Sprang right at Astur's face.
Through teeth, and skull, and helmet,
   So fierce a thrust he sped,
The good sword stood a hand-breadth out
   Behind the Tuscan's head.

46

And the great Lord of Luna
   Fell at that deadly stroke,
As falls on Mount Alvernus
   A thunder-smitten oak.
Far o'er the crashing forest
   The giant arms lie spread;
And the pale augurs, muttering low,
   Gaze on the blasted head.

47

On Astur's throat Horatius
   Right firmly pressed his heel,
And thrice and four times tugged amain,
   Ere he wrenched out the steel.
'And see,' he cried, 'the welcome,
   Fair guests, that waits you here!
What noble Lucumo comes next
   To taste our Roman cheer?'

48

But at his haughty challenge
 A sullen murmur ran,
Mingled of wrath, and shame, and dread,
 Along that glittering van.
There lacked not men of prowess,
 Nor men of lordly race;
For all Etruria's noblest
 Were round the fatal place.

49

But all Etruria's noblest
 Felt their hearts sink to see
On the earth the bloody corpses,
 In the path the dauntless Three:
And, from the ghastly entrance
 Where those bold Romans stood,
All shrank, like boys who unaware,
Ranging the woods to start a hare,
Come to the mouth of the dark lair
Where, growling low, a fierce old bear
 Lies amidst bones and blood.

50

Was none who would be foremost
 To lead such dire attack:
But those behind cried 'Forward!'
 And those before cried 'Back!'
And backward now and forward
 Wavers the deep array;
And on the tossing sea of steel,
To and fro the standards reel;
And the victorious trumpet-peal
 Dies fitfully away.

51

Yet one man for one moment
    Strode out before the crowd;
Well known was he to all the Three,
    And they gave him greeting loud.
'Now welcome, welcome, Sextus!
    Now welcome to thy home!
Why dost thou stay, and turn away?
    Here lies the road to Rome.'

52

Thrice looked he at the city;
    Thrice looked he at the dead;
And thrice came on in fury,
    And thrice turned back in dread:
And, white with fear and hatred,
    Scowled at the narrow way
Where, wallowing in a pool of blood,
    The bravest Tuscans lay.

53

But meanwhile axe and lever
    Have manfully been plied;
And now the bridge hangs tottering
    Above the boiling tide.
'Come back, come back, Horatius!'
    Loud cried the Fathers all.
'Back, Lartius! back, Herminius!
    Back, ere the ruin fall!'

54

Back darted Spurius Lartius;
    Herminius darted back:
And, as they passed, beneath their feet
    They felt the timbers crack.

But when they turned their faces,
    And on the farther shore
Saw brave Horatius stand alone,
    They would have crossed once more.

55

But with a crash like thunder
    Fell every loosened beam,
And, like a dam, the mighty wreck
    Lay right athwart the stream:
And a long shout of triumph
    Rose from the walls of Rome,
As to the highest turret-tops
    Was splashed the yellow foam.

56

And, like a horse unbroken
    When first he feels the rein,
The furious river struggled hard,
    And tossed his tawny mane,
And burst the curb and bounded,
    Rejoicing to be free,
And whirling down, in fierce career,
Battlement, and plank, and pier,
    Rushed headlong to the sea.

57

Alone stood brave Horatius,
    But constant still in mind;
Thrice thirty thousand foes before,
    And the broad flood behind.
'Down with him!' cried false Sextus,
    With a smile on his pale face.
'Now yield thee,' cried Lars Porsena,
    'Now yield thee to our grace.'

58

Round turned he, as not deigning
   Those craven ranks to see;
Nought spake he to Lars Porsena,
   To Sextus nought spake he;
But he saw on Palatinus
   The white porch of his home;
And he spake to the noble river
   That rolls by the towers of Rome.

59

'Oh, Tiber! father Tiber!
   To whom the Romans pray,
A Roman's life, a Roman's arms,
   Take thou in charge this day!'
So he spake, and speaking sheathed
   The good sword by his side,
And with his harness on his back,
   Plunged headlong in the tide.

60

No sound of joy or sorrow
   Was heard from either bank;
But friends and foes in dumb surprise,
With parted lips and straining eyes,
   Stood gazing where he sank;
And when above the surges
   They saw his crest appear,
All Rome sent forth a rapturous cry,
And even the ranks of Tuscany
   Could scarce forbear to cheer.

61

But fiercely ran the current,
   Swollen high by months of rain:
And fast his blood was flowing;
   And he was sore in pain,

And heavy with his armour,
   And spent with changing blows:
And oft they thought him sinking,
   But still again he rose.

62

Never, I ween, did swimmer,
   In such an evil case,
Struggle through such a raging flood
   Safe to the landing place:
But his limbs were borne up bravely
   By the brave heart within,
And our good father Tiber
   Bare bravely up his chin.

63

'Curse on him!' quoth false Sextus;
   'Will not the villain drown?
But for this stay, ere close of day
   We should have sacked the town!'
'Heaven help him!' quoth Lars Porsena,
   'And bring him safe to shore;
For such a gallant feat of arms
   Was never seen before.'

64

And now he feels the bottom;
   Now on dry earth he stands;
Now round him throng the Fathers;
   To press his gory hands;
And now with shouts and clapping,
   And noise of weeping loud,
He enters through the River-Gate,
   Borne by the joyous crowd.

65

They gave him of the corn-land,
    That was of public right,
As much as two strong oxen
    Could plough from morn till night;
And they made a molten image,
    And set it up on high,
And there it stands unto this day
    To witness if I lie.

66

It stands in the Comitium,
    Plain for all folk to see;
Horatius in his harness,
    Halting upon one knee:
And underneath is written,
    In letters all of gold,
How valiantly he kept the bridge
    In the brave days of old.

67

And still his name sounds stirring
    Unto the men of Rome,
As the trumpet-blast that cries to them
    To charge the Volscian home;
And wives still pray to Juno
    For boys with hearts as bold
As his who kept the bridge so well
    In the brave days of old.

68

And in the nights of winter,
    When the cold north winds blow,
And the long howling of the wolves
    Is heard amidst the snow;

When round the lonely cottage
   Roars loud the tempest's din,
And the good logs of Algidus
   Roar louder yet within;

69

When the oldest cask is opened,
   And the largest lamp is lit;
When the chestnuts glow in the embers,
   And the kid turns on the spit;
When young and old in circle
   Around the firebrands close;
When the girls are weaving baskets,
   And the lads are shaping bows;

70

When the goodman mends his armour,
   And trims his helmet's plume;
When the goodwife's shuttle merrily
   Goes flashing through the loom;
With weeping and with laughter
   Still is the story told,
How well Horatius kept the bridge
   In the brave days of old.

The Battle of the Lake Regillus

A LAY SUNG AT
THE FEAST OF CASTOR AND POLLUX
ON THE IDES OF QUINTILIS,
IN THE YEAR OF THE CITY CCCCLI

1

Ho, trumpets, sound a war-note!
　Ho, lictors, clear the way!
The Knights will ride, in all their pride,
　Along the streets today.
Today the doors and windows
　Are hung with garlands all,
From Castor in the Forum,
　To Mars without the wall.
Each Knight is robed in purple,
　With olive each is crowned;
A gallant war-horse under each
　Paws haughtily the ground.
While flows the Yellow River,
　While stands the Sacred Hill,
The proud Ides of Quintilis
　Shall have such honour still.
Gay are the Martian Kalends:
　December's Nones are gay:
But the proud Ides, when the squadron rides,
　Shall be Rome's whitest day.

2

Unto the Great Twin Brethren
　We keep this solemn feast.
Swift, swift, the Great Twin Brethren
　Came spurring from the east.
They came o'er wild Parthenius
　Tossing in waves of pine,
O'er Cirrha's dome, o'er Adria's foam,

O'er purple Apennine,
From where with flutes and dances
    Their ancient mansion rings,
In lordly Lacedæmon,
    The City of two kings,
To where, by Lake Regillus,
    Under the Porcian height,
All in the lands of Tusculum,
    Was fought the glorious fight.

3

Now on the place of slaughter
    Are cots and sheepfolds seen,
And rows of vines, and fields of wheat,
    And apple-orchards green:
The swine crush the big acorns
    That fall from Corne's oaks.
Upon the turf by the Fair Fount
    The reaper's pottage smokes.
The fisher baits his angle;
    The hunter twangs his bow;
Little they think on those strong limbs
    That moulder deep below.
Little they think how sternly
    That day the trumpets pealed;
How in the slippery swamp of blood
    Warrior and war-horse reeled;
How wolves came with fierce gallop,
    And crows on eager wings,
To tear the flesh of captains,
    And peck the eyes of kings;
How thick the dead lay scattered
    Under the Porcian height;
How through the gates of Tusculum
    Raved the wild stream of flight;
And how the Lake Regillus
    Bubbled with crimson foam,
What time the Thirty Cities
    Came forth to war with Rome.

4

But, Roman, when thou standest
    Upon that holy ground,
Look thou with heed on the dark rock
    That girds the dark lake round.
So shalt thou see a hoof-mark
    Stamped deep into the flint:
It was no hoof of mortal steed
    That made so strange a dint:
There to the Great Twin Brethren
    Vow thou thy vows, and pray
That they, in tempest and in fight,
    Will keep thy head alway.

5

Since last the Great Twin Brethren
    Of mortal eyes were seen,
Have years gone by an hundred
    And fourscore and thirteen.
That summer a Virginius
    Was Consul first in place;
The second was stout Aulus,
    Of the Posthumian race.
The Herald of the Latines
    From Gabii came in state.
The Herald of the Latines
    Passed through Rome's Eastern Gate:
The Herald of the Latines
    Did in our Forum stand;
And there he did his office,
    A sceptre in his hand.

6

'Hear, Senators and people
    Of the good town of Rome:
The Thirty Cities charge you
    To bring the Tarquins home:
And if ye still be stubborn,

To work the Tarquins wrong,
The Thirty Cities warn you,
   Look that your walls be strong.'

7

Then spake the Consul Aulus,
   He spake a bitter jest:
'Once the jays sent a message
   Unto the eagle's nest: –
Now yield thou up thine eyrie
   Unto the carrion-kite,
Or come forth valiantly, and face
   The jays in deadly fight. –
Forth looked in wrath the eagle;
   And carrion-kite and jay,
Soon as they saw his beak and claw,
   Fled screaming far away.'

8

The Herald of the Latines
   Hath hied him back in state:
The Fathers of the City
   Are met in high debate.
Then spake the elder Consul,
   An ancient man and wise:
'Now hearken, Conscript Fathers,
   To that which I advise.
In seasons of great peril
   'Tis good that one bear sway;
Then choose we a Dictator,
   Whom all men shall obey.
Camerium knows how deeply
   The sword of Aulus bites
And all our city calls him
   The man of seventy fights.
Then let him be Dictator
   For six months and no more,
And have a Master of the Knights,
   And axes twenty-four.'

9

So Aulus was Dictator,
  The man of seventy fights;
He made Æbutius Elva
  His Master of the Knights.
On the third morn thereafter,
  At dawning of the day,
Did Aulus and Æbutius
  Set forth with their array.
Sempronius Atratinus
  Was left in charge at home
With boys, and with grey-headed men,
  To keep the walls of Rome.
Hard by the Lake Regillus
  Our camp was pitched at night:
Eastward a mile the Latines lay,
  Under the Porcian height.
Far over hill and valley
  Their mighty host was spread;
And with their thousand watch-fires
  The midnight sky was red.

10

Up rose the golden morning
  Over the Porcian height,
The proud Ides of Quintilis
  Marked evermore with white.
Not without secret trouble
  Our bravest saw the foes;
For girt by threescore thousand spears,
  The thirty standards rose.
From every warlike city
  That boasts the Latian name,
Foredoomed to dogs and vultures,
  That gallant army came;
From Setia's purple vineyards,
  From Norba's ancient wall,
From the white streets of Tusculum,
  The proudest town of all;

From where the Witch's Fortress
    O'erhangs the dark-blue seas;
From the still glassy lake that sleeps
    Beneath Aricia's trees –
Those trees in whose dim shadow
    The ghastly priest doth reign,
The priest who slew the slayer,
    And shall himself be slain;
From the drear banks of Ufens,
    Where flights of marsh-fowl play,
And buffaloes lie wallowing
    Through the hot summer's day;
From the gigantic watch-towers,
    No work of earthly men,
Whence Cora's sentinels o'erlook
    The never-ending fen;
From the Laurentian jungle,
    The wild hog's reedy home;
From the green steeps whence Anio leaps
    In floods of snow-white foam.

11

Aricia, Cora, Norba,
    Velitræ, with the might
Of Setia and of Tusculum,
    Were marshalled on the right:
Their leader was Mamilius,
    Prince of the Latian name;
Upon his head a helmet
    Of red gold shone like flame:
High on a gallant charger
    Of dark-grey hue he rode;
Over his gilded armour
    A vest of purple flowed,
Woven in the land of sunrise
    By Syria's dark-browed daughters,
And by the sails of Carthage brought
    Far o'er the southern waters.

12

Lavinium and Laurentum
  Had on the left their post,
With all the banners of the marsh,
  And banners of the coast.
Their leader was false Sextus,
  That wrought the deed of shame:
With restless pace and haggard face,
  To his last field he came.
Men said he saw strange visions
  Which none beside might see;
And that strange sounds were in his ears
  Which none might hear but he.
A woman fair and stately,
  But pale as are the dead,
Oft through the watches of the night
  Sat spinning by his bed.
And as she plied the distaff,
  In a sweet voice and low,
She sang of great old houses,
  And fights fought long ago.
So spun she, and so sang she,
  Until the east was grey;
Then pointed to her bleeding breast,
  And shrieked, and fled away.

13

But in the centre thickest
  Were ranged the shields of foes,
And from the centre loudest
  The cry of battle rose.
There Tibur marched and Pedum
  Beneath proud Tarquin's rule,
And Ferentinum of the rock,
  And Gabii of the pool.
There rode the Volscian succours:
  There, in a dark stern ring,
The Roman exiles gathered close
  Around the ancient king.

Though white as Mount Soracte,
    When winter nights are long,
His beard flowed down o'er mail and belt,
    His heart and hand were strong:
Under his hoary eyebrows
    Still flashed forth quenchless rage:
And, if the lance shook in his gripe,
    'Twas more with hate than age.
Close at his side was Titus
    On an Apulian steed,
Titus, the youngest Tarquin,
    Too good for such a breed.

14

Now on each side the leaders
    Gave signal for the charge;
And on each side the footmen
    Strode on with lance and targe;
And on each side the horsemen
    Struck their spurs deep in gore
And front to front the armies
    Met with a mighty roar:
And under that great battle
    The earth with blood was red;
And, like the Pomptine fog at morn,
    The dust hung overhead;
And louder still and louder
    Rose from the darkened field
The braying of the war-horns,
    The clang of sword and shield,
The rush of squadrons sweeping
    Like whirlwinds o'er the plain,
The shouting of the slayers,
    And screeching of the slain.

15

False Sextus rode out foremost,
  His look was high and bold;
His corslet was of bison's hide,
  Plated with steel and gold.
As glares the famished eagle
  From the Digentian rock
On a choice lamb that bounds alone
  Before Bandusia's flock,
Herminius glared on Sextus,
  And came with eagle speed,
Herminius on black Auster,
  Brave champion on brave steed;
In his right hand the broadsword
  That kept the bridge so well,
And on his helm the crown he won
  When proud Fidenæ fell.
Woe to the maid whose lover
  Shall cross his path today!
False Sextus saw, and trembled,
  And turned, and fled away.
As turns, as flies, the woodman
  In the Calabrian brake,
When through the reeds gleams the round eye
  Of that fell painted snake;
So turned, so fled, false Sextus,
  And hid him in the rear,
Behind the dark Lavinian ranks,
  Bristling with crest and spear.

16

Then far to north Æbutius,
  The Master of the Knights,
Gave Tubero of Norba
  To feed the Porcian kites.
Next under those red horse-hoofs
  Flaccus of Setia lay;
Better had he been pruning
  Among his elms that day.

Mamilius saw the slaughter,
  And tossed his golden crest,
And towards the Master of the Knights
  Through the thick battle pressed.
Æbutius smote Mamilius
  So fiercely on the shield
That the great lord of Tusculum
  Well nigh rolled on the field.
Mamilius smote Æbutius,
  With a good aim and true,
Just where the neck and shoulder join,
  And pierced him through and through;
And brave Æbutius Elva
  Fell swooning to the ground:
But a thick wall of bucklers
  Encompassed him around.
His clients from the battle
  Bare him some little space,
And filled a helm from the dark lake,
  And bathed his brow and face;
And when at last he opened
  His swimming eyes to light,
Men say, the earliest words he spake
  Was, 'Friends, how goes the fight?'

17

But meanwhile in the centre
  Great deeds of arms were wrought;
There Aulus the Dictator
  And there Valerius fought.
Aulus with his good broadsword
  A bloody passage cleared
To where, amidst the thickest foes,
  He saw the long white beard.
Flat lighted that good broadsword
  Upon proud Tarquin's head.
He dropped the lance: he dropped the reins:
  He fell as fall the dead.
Down Aulus springs to slay him,
  With eyes like coals of fire;

But faster Titus hath sprung down,
  And hath bestrode his sire.
Latian captains, Roman knights,
  Fast down to earth they spring,
And hand to hand they fight on foot
  Around the ancient king.
First Titus gave tall Cæso
  A death wound in the face;
Tall Cæso was the bravest man
  Of the brave Fabian race:
Aulus slew Rex of Gabii,
  The priest of Juno's shrine:
Valerius smote down Julius,
  Of Rome's great Julian line;
Julius, who left his mansion,
  High on the Velian hill,
And through all turns of weal and woe
  Followed proud Tarquin still.
Now right across proud Tarquin
  A corpse was Julius laid;
And Titus groaned with rage and grief,
  And at Valerius made.
Valerius struck at Titus,
  And lopped off half his crest;
But Titus stabbed Valerius
  A span deep in the breast.
Like a mast snapped by the tempest,
  Valerius reeled and fell.
Ah! woe is me for the good house
  That loves the people well!
Then shouted loud the Latines;
  And with one rush they bore
The struggling Romans backward
  Three lances' length and more:
And up they took proud Tarquin,
  And laid him on a shield,
And four strong yeomen bare him,
  Still senseless, from the field.

18

But fiercer grew the fighting
   Around Valerius dead;
For Titus dragged him by the foot
And Aulus by the head.
'On, Latines, on!' quoth Titus,
   'See how the rebels fly!'
'Romans, stand firm!' quoth Aulus,
   'And win this fight or die!
They must not give Valerius
   To raven and to kite;
For aye Valerius loathed the wrong,
   And aye upheld the right:
And for your wives and babies
   In the front rank he fell.
Now play the men for the good house
   That loves the people well!'

19

Then tenfold round the body
   The roar of battle rose,
Like the roar of a burning forest,
   When a strong north wind blows.
Now backward, and now forward,
   Rocked furiously the fray,
Till none could see Valerius,
   And none wist where he lay.
For shivered arms and ensigns
   Were heaped there in a mound,
And corpses stiff, and dying men
   That writhed and gnawed the ground;
And wounded horses kicking,
   And snorting purple foam:
Right well did such a couch befit
   A Consular of Rome.

20

But north looked the Dictator;
   North looked he long and hard,
And spake to Caius Cossus,
   The Captain of his Guard;
'Caius, of all the Romans
   Thou hast the keenest sight,
Say, what through yonder storm of dust
   Comes from the Latian right?'

21

Then answered Caius Cossus:
   'I see an evil sight;
The banner of proud Tusculum
   Comes from the Latian right;
I see the plumed horsemen;
   And far before the rest
I see the dark-grey charger,
   I see the purple vest;
I see the golden helmet
   That shines far off like flame;
So ever rides Mamilius,
   Prince of the Latian name.'

22

'Now hearken, Caius Cossus:
   Spring on thy horse's back;
Ride as the wolves of Apennine
   Were all upon thy track;
Haste to our southward battle
   And never draw thy rein
Until thou find Herminius,
   And bid him come amain.'

23

So Aulus spake, and turned him
  Again to that fierce strife;
And Caius Cossus mounted,
  And rode for death and life.
Loud clanged beneath his horse-hoofs
  The helmets of the dead,
And many a curdling pool of blood
  Splashed him from heel to head.
So came he far to southward,
  Where fought the Roman host,
Against the banners of the marsh
  And banners of the coast.
Like corn before the sickle
  The stout Lavinians fell,
Beneath the edge of the true sword
  That kept the bridge so well.

24

'Herminius! Aulus greets thee;
  He bids thee come with speed,
To help our central battle;
  For sore is there our need.
There wars the youngest Tarquin,
  And there the Crest of Flame,
The Tusculan Mamilius,
  Prince of the Latian name.
Valerius hath fallen fighting
  In front of our array;
And Aulus of the seventy fields
  Alone upholds the day.'

25

Herminius beat his bosom;
  But never a word he spake.
He clapped his hand on Auster's mane;
  He gave the reins a shake,

Away, away, went Auster,
    Like an arrow from the bow:
Black Auster was the fleetest steed
    From Aufidus to Po.

26

Right glad were all the Romans
    Who, in that hour of dread,
Against great odds bare up the war
    Around Valerius dead,
When from the south the cheering
    Rose with a mighty swell;
'Herminius comes, Herminius,
    Who kept the bridge so well!'

27

Mamilius spied Herminius,
    And dashed across the way.
'Herminius! I have sought thee
    Through many a bloody day.
One of us two, Herminius,
    Shall never more go home.
I will lay on for Tusculum,
    And lay thou on for Rome!'

28

All round them paused the battle,
    While met in mortal fray
The Roman and the Tusculan,
    The horses black and grey.
Herminius smote Mamilius
    Through breast-plate and through breast,
And fast flowed out the purple blood
    Over the purple vest.
Mamilius smote Herminius
    Through head-piece and through head;
And side by side those chiefs of pride
    Together fell down dead.

Down fell they dead together
   In a great lake of gore;
And still stood all who saw them fall
   While men might count a score.

29

Fast, fast, with heels wild spurning,
   The dark-grey charger fled:
He burst through ranks of fighting men;
   He sprang o'er heaps of dead.
His bridle far out-streaming,
   His flanks all blood and foam,
He sought the southern mountains,
   The mountains of his home.
The pass was steep and rugged,
   The wolves they howled and whined;
But he ran like a whirlwind up the pass,
   And he left the wolves behind.
Through many a startled hamlet
   Thundered his flying feet:
He rushed through the gate of Tusculum,
   He rushed up the long white street;
He rushed by tower and temple,
   And paused not from his race
Till he stood before his master's door
   In the stately market-place.
And straightway round him gathered
   A pale and trembling crowd,
And when they knew him, cries of rage
   Brake forth, and wailing loud:
And women rent their tresses
   For their great prince's fall;
And old men girt on their old swords,
   And went to man the wall.

30

But, like a graven image,
  Black Auster kept his place,
And ever wistfully he looked
  Into his master's face.
The raven-mane that daily,
  With pats and fond caresses,
The young Herminia washed and combed,
  And twined in even tresses,
And decked with coloured ribands
  From her own gay attire,
Hung sadly o'er her father's corpse
  In carnage and in mire.
Forth with a shout sprang Titus,
  And seized black Auster's rein.
Then Aulus sware a fearful oath,
  And ran at him amain.
'The furies of thy brother
  With me and mine abide,
If one of your accursed house
  Upon black Auster ride!'
As on an Alpine watch-tower
  From heaven comes down the flame,
Full on the neck of Titus
  The blade of Aulus came:
And out the red blood spouted,
  In a wide arch and tall,
As spouts a fountain in the court
  Of some rich Capuan's hall.
The knees of all the Latines
  Were loosened with dismay,
When dead, on dead Herminius,
  The bravest Tarquin lay.

31

And Aulus the Dictator
  Stroked Auster's raven mane,
With heed he looked unto the girths,
  With heed unto the rein.

'Now bear me well, black Auster,
    Into yon thick array;
And thou and I will have revenge
    For thy good lord this day.'

32

So spake he; and was buckling
    Tighter black Auster's band,
When he was aware of a princely pair
    That rode at his right hand.
So like they were, no mortal
    Might one from other know:
White as snow their armour was:
    Their steeds were white as snow.
Never on earthly anvil
    Did such rare armour gleam;
And never did such gallant steeds
    Drink of an earthly stream.

33

And all who saw them trembled,
    And pale grew every cheek;
And Aulus the Dictator
    Scarce gathered voice to speak.
'Say by what name men call you?
    What city is your home?
And wherefore ride ye in such guise
    Before the ranks of Rome?'

34

'By many names men call us;
    In many lands we dwell:
Well Samothracia knows us;
    Cyrene knows us well.
Our house in gay Tarentum
    Is hung each morn with flowers:
High o'er the masts of Syracuse
    Our marble portal towers;

But by the proud Eurotas
  Is our dear native home;
And for the right we come to fight
  Before the ranks of Rome.'

35

So answered those strange horsemen,
  And each couched low his spear;
And forthwith all the ranks of Rome
  Were bold, and of good cheer:
And on the thirty armies
  Came wonder and affright,
And Ardea wavered on the left,
  And Cora on the right.
'Rome to the charge!' cried Aulus;
  'The foe begins to yield!
Charge for the hearth of Vesta!
  Charge for the Golden Shield!
Let no man stop to plunder,
  But slay, and slay, and slay;
The Gods who live for ever
  Are on our side today.'

36

Then the fierce trumpet-flourish
  From earth to heaven arose,
The kites know well the long stern swell
  That bids the Romans close.
Then the good sword of Aulus
  Was lifted up to slay:
Then, like a crag down Apennine,
  Rushed Auster through the fray.
But under those strange horsemen
  Still thicker lay the slain;
And after those strange horses
  Black Auster toiled in vain.
Behind them Rome's long battle
  Came rolling on the foe,

Ensigns dancing wild above,
    Blades all in line below.
So comes the Po in flood-time
    Upon the Celtic plain:
So comes the squall, blacker than night,
    Upon the Adrian main.
Now, by our Sire Quirinus,
    It was a goodly sight
To see the thirty standards
    Swept down the tide of flight.
So flies the spray of Adria
    When the black squall doth blow,
So corn-sheaves in the flood-time
    Spin down the whirling Po.
False Sextus to the mountains
    Turned first his horse's head;
And fast fled Ferentinum,
    And fast Lanuvium fled.
The horsemen of Nomentum
    Spurred hard out of the fray;
The footmen of Velitræ
    Threw shield and spear away.
And underfoot was trampled,
    Amidst the mud and gore,
The banner of proud Tusculum,
    That never stooped before:
And down went Flavius Faustus,
    Who led his stately ranks
From where the apple blossoms wave
    On Anio's echoing banks,
And Tullus of Arpinum,
    Chief of the Volscian aids,
And Metius with the long fair curls,
    The love of Anxur's maids,
And the white head of Vulso,
    The great Arician seer,
And Nepos of Laurentum,
    The hunter of the deer;
And in the back false Sextus
    Felt the good Roman steel,

And wriggling in the dust he died,
    Like a worm beneath the wheel:
And fliers and pursuers
    Were mingled in a mass;
And far away the battle
    Went roaring through the pass.

37

Sempronius Atratinus
    Sat in the Eastern Gate,
Beside him were three Fathers,
    Each in his chair of state;
Fabius, whose nine stout grandsons
    That day were in the field,
And Manlius, eldest of the Twelve
    Who keep the Golden Shield;
And Sergius, the High Pontiff,
    For wisdom far renowned;
In all Etruria's colleges
    Was no such Pontiff found.
And all around the portal,
    And high above the wall,
Stood a great throng of people,
    But sad and silent all;
Young lads, and stooping elders
    That might not bear the mail,
Matrons with lips that quivered,
    And maids with faces pale.
Since the first gleam of daylight,
    Sempronius had not ceased
To listen for the rushing
    Of horse-hoofs from the east.
The mist of eve was rising,
    The sun was hastening down,
When he was aware of a princely pair
    Fast pricking towards the town.
So like they were, man never
    Saw twins so like before;
Red with gore their armour was,
    Their steeds were red with gore.

38

'Hail to the great Asylum!
   Hail to the hill-tops seven!
Hail to the fire that burns for aye,
   And the shield that fell from heaven!
This day, by Lake Regillus,
   Under the Porcian height,
All in the lands of Tusculum
   Was fought a glorious fight.
Tomorrow your Dictator
   Shall bring in triumph home
The spoils of thirty cities
   To deck the shrines of Rome!'

39

Then burst from that great concourse
   A shout that shook the towers,
And some ran north, and some ran south,
   Crying, 'The day is ours!'
But on rode these strange horsemen,
   With slow and lordly pace;
And none who saw their bearing
   Durst ask their name or race.
On rode they to the Forum,
   While laurel-boughs and flowers,
From house-tops and from windows,
   Fell on their crests in showers.
When they drew nigh to Vesta,
   They vaulted down amain,
And washed their horses in the well
   That springs by Vesta's fane.
And straight again they mounted,
   And rode to Vesta's door;
Then, like a blast, away they passed,
   And no man saw them more.

40

And all the people trembled,
  And pale grew every cheek;
And Sergius the High Pontiff
  Alone found voice to speak:
'The Gods who live for ever
  Have fought for Rome today!
These be the Great Twin Brethren
  To whom the Dorians pray.
Back comes the Chief in triumph,
  Who, in the hour of fight,
Hath seen the Great Twin Brethren
  In harness on his right.
Safe comes the ship to haven,
  Through billows and through gales,
If once the Great Twin Brethren
  Sit shining on the sails.
Wherefore they washed their horses
  In Vesta's holy well,
Wherefore they rode to Vesta's door,
  I know, but may not tell.
Here, hard by Vesta's temple,
  Build we a stately dome
Unto the Great Twin Brethren
  Who fought so well for Rome.
And when the months returning
  Bring back this day of fight,
The proud Ides of Quintilis,
  Marked evermore with white,
Unto the Great Twin Brethren
  Let all the people throng,
With chaplets and with offerings,
  With music and with song;
And let the doors and windows
  Be hung with garlands all,
And let the Knights be summoned
  To Mars without the wall:
Thence let them ride in purple
  With joyous trumpet-sound,

Each mounted on his war-horse,
  And each with olive crowned;
And pass in solemn order
  Before the sacred dome,
Where dwell the Great Twin Brethren
  Who fought so well for Rome.'

Virginia

**FRAGMENTS OF A LAY SUNG IN THE FORUM ON THE DAY
WHEREON LUCIUS SEXTIUS SEXTINUS LATERANUS AND
CAIUS LICINIUS CALVUS STOLO WERE ELECTED TRIBUNES
OF THE COMMONS THE FIFTH TIME, IN THE YEAR OF
THE CITY CCCLXXXII**

Ye good men of the Commons, with loving hearts and true,
Who stand by the bold Tribunes that still have stood by you,
Come, make a circle round me, and mark my tale with care,
A tale of what Rome once hath borne, of what Rome yet may
    bear.
This is no Grecian fable, of fountains running wine,
Of maids with snaky tresses, or sailors turned to swine.
Here, in this very Forum, under the noonday sun,
In sight of all the people, the bloody deed was done
Old men still creep among us who saw that fearful day,
Just seventy years and seven ago, when the wicked Ten bare
    sway.

Of all the wicked Ten still the names are held accursed,
And of all the wicked Ten Appius Claudius was the worst.
He stalked along the Forum like King Tarquin in his pride:
Twelve axes waited on him, six marching on a side;
The townsmen shrank to right and left, and eyed askance
    with fear
His lowering brow, his curling mouth which always seemed
    to sneer.
That brow of hate, that mouth of scorn, marks all the
    kindred still;
For never was there Claudius yet but wished the Commons
    ill:
Nor lacks he fit attendance; for close behind his heels,
With outstretched chin and crouching pace, the client
    Marcus steals,

His loins girt up to run with speed, be the errand what
   it may,
And the smile flickering on his cheek, for aught his lord
   may say.
Such varlets pimp and jest for hire among the lying Greeks:
Such varlets still are paid to hoot when brave Licinius speaks.
Where'er ye shed the honey, the buzzing flies will crowd;
Where'er ye fling the carrion, the raven's croak is loud;
Where'er down Tiber garbage floats, the greedy pike ye see;
And wheresoe'er such lord is found, such client still will be.

   Just then, as through one cloudless chink in a black
      stormy sky
Shines out the dewy morning-star, a fair young girl came by.
With her small tablets in her hand, and her satchel on her
   arm,
Home she went bounding from the school, nor dreamed of
   shame or harm;
And past those dreaded axes she innocently ran,
With bright, frank brow that had not learned to blush at gaze
   of man;
And up the Sacred Street she turned, and, as she danced
   along,
She warbled gaily to herself lines of the good old song,
How for a sport the princes came spurring from the camp,
And found Lucrece, combing the fleece, under the midnight
   lamp.
The maiden sang as sings the lark, when up he darts his
   flight,
From his nest in the green April corn, to meet the morning
   light;
And Appius heard her sweet young voice, and saw her sweet
   young face,
And loved her with the accursed love of his accursed race,
And all along the Forum, and up the Sacred Street,
His vulture eye pursued the trip of those small glancing feet.

   Over the Alban mountains the light of morning broke;
From all the roofs of the Seven Hills curled the thin wreaths
   of smoke:

The city-gates were opened; the Forum all alive,
With buyers and with sellers was humming like a hive:
Blithely on brass and timber the craftsman's stroke was
    ringing,
And blithely o'er her panniers the market-girl was singing,
And blithely young Virginia came smiling from her home:
Ah! woe for young Virginia, the sweetest maid in Rome!
With her small tablets in her hand, and her satchel on her
    arm,
Forth she went bounding to the school, nor dreamed of
    shame or harm.
She crossed the Forum shining with stalls in alleys gay,
And just had reached the very spot whereon I stand this day,
When up the varlet Marcus came; not such as when erewhile
He crouched behind his patron's heels with the true client
    smile:
He came with lowering forehead, swollen features, and
    clenched fist,
And strode across Virginia's path, and caught her by the
    wrist.
Hard strove the frighted maiden, and screamed with look
    aghast;
And at her scream from right and left the folk came running
    fast;
The money-changer Crispus, with his thin silver hairs,
And Hanno from the stately booth glittering with Punic
    wares,
And the strong smith Muræna, grasping a half-forged brand,
And Volero the flesher, his cleaver in his hand.
All came in wrath and wonder; for all knew that fair child;
And, as she passed them twice a day, all kissed their hands
    and smiled;
And the strong smith Muræna gave Marcus such a blow,
The caitiff reeled three paces back, and let the maiden go.
Yet glared he fiercely round him, and growled in harsh, fell
    tone,
'She's mine, and I will have her: I seek but for mine own:
She is my slave, born in my house, and stolen away and sold,
The year of the sore sickness, ere she was twelve hours old.
'Twas in the sad September, the month of wail and fright,

Two augurs were borne forth that morn; the Consul died ere
    night.
I wait on Appius Claudius, I waited on his sire:
Let him who works the client wrong beware the patron's ire!'

    So spake the varlet Marcus; and dread and silence came
On all the people at the sound of the great Claudian name.
For then there was no Tribune to speak the word of might,
Which makes the rich man tremble, and guards the poor
    man's right.
There was no brave Licinius, no honest Sextius then;
But all the city, in great fear, obeyed the wicked Ten.
Yet ere the varlet Marcus again might seize the maid,
Who clung tight to Muræna's skirt, and sobbed, and
    shrieked for aid,
Forth through the throng of gazers the young Icilius pressed,
And stamped his foot, and rent his gown, and smote upon
    his breast,
And sprang upon that column, by many a minstrel sung,
Whereon three mouldering helmets, three rusting swords, are
    hung,
And beckoned to the people, and in bold voice and clear
Poured thick and fast the burning words which tyrants quake
    to hear.

    'Now, by your children's cradles, now by your fathers'
    graves,
Be men today, Quirites, or be for ever slaves!
For this did Servius give us laws? For this did Lucrece bleed?
For this was the great vengeance wrought on Tarquin's evil
    seed?
For this did those false sons make red the axes of their sire?
For this did Scævola's right hand hiss in the Tuscan fire?
Shall the vile fox-earth awe the race that stormed the lion's
    den?
Shall we, who could not brook one lord, crouch to the
    wicked Ten?
Oh for that ancient spirit which curbed the Senate's will!
Oh for the tents which in old time whitened the Sacred Hill!
In those brave days our fathers stood firmly side by side;

They faced the Marcian fury; they tamed the Fabian pride:
They drove the fiercest Quinctius an outcast forth from Rome;
They sent the haughtiest Claudius with shivered fasces home.
But what their care bequeathed us our madness flung away:
All the ripe fruit of threescore years was blighted in a day.
Exult, ye proud Patricians! The hard-fought fight is o'er.
We strove for honours – 'twas in vain: for freedom – 'tis no
      more.
No crier to the polling summons the eager throng;
No tribune breathes the word of might that guards the weak
      from wrong.
Our very hearts, that were so high, sink down beneath your
      will.
Riches, and lands, and power, and state – ye have them: –
      keep them still.
Still keep the holy fillets; still keep the purple gown,
The axes, and the curule chair, the car, and laurel crown:
Still press us for your cohorts, and, when the fight is done,
Still fill your garners from the soil which our good swords
      have won.
Still, like a spreading ulcer, which leech-craft may not cure,
Let your foul usance eat away the substance of the poor.
Still let your haggard debtors bear all their fathers bore;
Still let your dens of torment be noisome as of yore;
No fire when Tiber freezes; no air in dog star heat;
And store of rods for free-born backs, and holes for free-born
      feet.
Heap heavier still the fetters; bar closer still the grate;
Patient as sheep we yield us up unto your cruel hate.
But, by the Shades beneath us, and by the Gods above,
Add not unto your cruel hate your yet more cruel love!
Have ye not graceful ladies, whose spotless lineage springs
From Consuls, and High Pontiffs, and ancient Alban kings?
Ladies, who deign not on our paths to set their tender feet,
Who from their cars look down with scorn upon the
      wondering street,
Who in Corinthian mirrors their own proud smiles behold,
And breathe of Capuan odours, and shine with Spanish gold?
Then leave the poor Plebeian his single tie to life –
The sweet, sweet love of daughter, of sister, and of wife,

The gentle speech, the balm for all that his vexed soul
    endures,
The kiss, in which he half forgets even such a yoke as yours.
Still let the maiden's beauty swell the father's breast with
    pride;
Still let the bridegroom's arms infold an unpolluted bride.
Spare us the inexpiable wrong, the unutterable shame,
That turns the coward's heart to steel, the sluggard's blood to
    flame,
Lest, when our latest hope is fled, ye taste of our despair,
And learn by proof, in some wild hour, how much the
    wretched dare.'

   Straightway Virginius led the maid a little space aside,
To where the reeking shambles stood, piled up with horn
    and hide,
Close to yon low dark archway, where, in a crimson flood,
Leaps down to the great sewer the gurgling stream of blood.
Hard by, a flesher on a block had laid his whittle down:
Virginius caught the whittle up, and hid it in his gown.
And then his eyes grew very dim, and his throat began to
    swell,
And in a hoarse, changed voice he spake, 'Farewell, sweet
    child! Farewell!
Oh! how I loved my darling! Though stern I sometimes be,
To thee, thou know'st, I was not so. Who could be so to
    thee?
And how my darling loved me! How glad she was to hear
My footstep on the threshold when I came back last year!
And how she danced with pleasure to see my civic crown,
And took my sword, and hung it up, and brought me forth
    my gown!
Now, all those things are over – yes, all thy pretty ways,
Thy needlework, thy prattle, thy snatches of old lays;
And none will grieve when I go forth, or smile when I return,
Or watch beside the old man's bed, or weep upon his urn.
The house that was the happiest within the Roman walls,
The house that envied not the wealth of Capua's marble
    halls,

Now, for the brightness of thy smile, must have eternal
    gloom,
And for the music of thy voice, the silence of the tomb.
The time is come. See how he points his eager hand this way!
See how his eyes gloat on thy grief, like a kite's upon the prey!
With all his wit, he little deems, that, spurned, betrayed,
    bereft,
Thy father hath in his despair one fearful refuge left.
He little deems that in this hand I clutch what still can save
Thy gentle youth from taunts and blows, the portion of the
    slave;
Yea, and from nameless evil, that passeth taunt and blow –
Foul outrage which thou knowest not, which thou shalt
    never know.
Then clasp me round the neck once more, and give me one
    more kiss;
And now mine own dear little girl, there is no way but this.'
With that he lifted high the steel, and smote her in the side,
And in her blood she sank to earth, and with one sob she
    died.

Then, for a little moment, all people held their breath;
And through the crowded Forum was stillness as of death;
And in another moment brake forth from one and all
A cry as if the Volscians were coming o'er the wall.
Some with averted faces shrieking fled home amain;
Some ran to call a leech; and some ran to lift the slain:
Some felt her lips and little wrist, if life might there be found;
And some tore up their garments fast, and strove to stanch
    the wound.
In vain they ran, and felt, and stanched; for never truer blow
That good right arm had dealt in fight against a Volscian foe.

When Appius Claudius saw that deed, he shuddered and
    sank down,
And hid his face some little space with the corner of his
    gown,
Till, with white lips and bloodshot eyes, Virginius tottered
    nigh,

And stood before the judgment-seat, and held the knife on
 high.
'Oh! dwellers in the nether gloom, avengers of the slain,
By this dear blood I cry to you, do right between us twain;
And even as Appius Claudius hath dealt by me and mine,
Deal you by Appius Claudius and all the Claudian line!'
So spake the slayer of his child, and turned, and went his
 way;
But first he cast one haggard glance to where the body lay,
And writhed, and groaned a fearful groan, and then, with
 steadfast feet,
Strode right across the market-place unto the Sacred Street.

Then up sprang Appius Claudius: 'Stop him; alive or dead!
Ten thousand pounds of copper to the man who brings his
 head.'
He looked upon his clients; but none would work his will.
He looked upon his lictors; but they trembled, and stood
 still.
And, as Virginius through the press his way in silence cleft,
Ever the mighty multitude fell back to right and left.
And he hath passed in safety unto his woeful home,
And there ta'en horse to tell the camp what deeds are done
 in Rome.

 By this the flood of people was swollen from every side,
And streets and porches round were filled with that
 o'erflowing tide;
And close around the body gathered a little train
Of them that were the nearest and dearest to the slain.
They brought a bier, and hung it with many a cypress crown,
And gently they uplifted her, and gently laid her down.
The face of Appius Claudius wore the Claudian scowl and
 sneer,
And in the Claudian note he cried, 'What doth this rabble
 here?
Have they no crafts to mind at home, that hitherward they
 stray?
Ho! lictors, clear the market-place, and fetch the corpse
 away!'

The voice of grief and fury till then had not been loud;
But a deep sullen murmur wandered among the crowd,
Like the moaning noise that goes before the whirlwind on the
 deep,
Or the growl of a fierce watch-dog but half-aroused from
 sleep.
But when the lictors at that word, tall yeomen all and strong,
Each with his axe and sheaf of twigs, went down into the
 throng,
Those old men say, who saw that day of sorrow and of sin,
That in the Roman Forum was never such a din.
The wailing, hooting, cursing, the howls of grief and hate,
Were heard beyond the Pincian Hill, beyond the Latin Gate.
But close around the body, where stood the little train
Of them that were the nearest and dearest to the slain,
No cries were there, but teeth set fast, low whispers and
 black frowns,
And breaking up of benches, and girding up of gowns.
'Twas well the lictors might not pierce to where the maiden
 lay,
Else surely had they been all twelve torn limb from limb that
 day.
Right glad they were to struggle back, blood streaming from
 their heads,
With axes all in splinters, and raimen all in shreds.
Then Appius Claudius gnawed his lip, and the blood left his
 cheek;
And thrice he beckoned with his hand, and thrice he strove
 to speak;
And thrice the tossing Forum set up a frightful yell;
"See, see, thou dog! what thou hast done; and hide thy
 shame in hell!
Thou that wouldt make our maidens slaves must first make
 slaves of men.
Tribunes! Hurrah for Tribunes! Down with the wicked Ten!'
And straightway, thick as hailstones, came whizzing through
 the air,
Pebbles, and bricks, and potsherds, all round the curule
 chair:
And upon Appius Claudius great fear and trembling came,

For never was a Claudius yet brave against aught but shame.
Though the great houses love us not, we own, to do them
     right,
That the great houses, all save one, have borne them well in
     fight.
Still Caius of Corioli, his triumphs and his wrongs,
His vengeance and his mercy, live in our camp-fire songs.
Beneath the yoke of Furius oft have Gaul and Tusca bowed;
And Rome may bear the pride of him of whom herself is
     proud.
But evermore a Claudius shrinks from a stricken field,
And changes colour like a maid at sight of sword and shield.
The Claudian triumphs all were won within the city towers;
The Claudian yoke was never pressed on any necks but ours.
A Cossus, like a wild cat, springs ever at the face;
A Fabius rushes like a boar against the shouting chase;
But the vile Claudian litter, raging with currish spite,
Still yelps and snaps at those who run, still runs from those
     who smite.
So now 'twas seen of Appius. When stones began to fly,
He shook, and crouched, and wrung his hands, and smote
     upon his thigh.
'Kind clients, honest lictors, stand by me in this fray!
Must I be torn in pieces? Home, home, the nearest way!'
While yet he spake, and looked around with a bewildered
     stare,
Four sturdy lictors put their necks beneath the curule chair;
And fourscore clients on the left, and fourscore on the right,
Arrayed themselves with swords and staves, and loins girt up
     for fight.
But, though without or staff or sword, so furious was the
     throng,
That scarce the train with might and main could bring their
     lord along.
Twelve times the crowd made at him; five times they seized
     his gown;
Small chance was his to rise again, if once they got him
     down:
And sharper came the pelting; and evermore the yell –
'Tribunes! we will have Tribunes!' – rose with a louder swell:

And the chair tossed as tosses a bark with tattered sail
When raves the Adriatic beneath an eastern gale,
When the Calabrian sea-marks are lost in clouds of spume,
And the great Thunder-Cape has donned his veil of inky
    gloom.
One stone hit Appius in the mouth, and one beneath the ear;
And ere he reached Mount Palatine, he swooned with pain
    and fear.
His cursed head, that he was wont to hold so high with
    pride,
Now, like a drunken man's, hung down, and swayed from
    side to side;
And when his stout retainers had brought him to his door,
His face and neck were all one cake of filth and clotted gore.
As Appius Claudius was that day, so may his grandson be!
God send Rome one such other sight, and send me there to
    see!

The Prophecy of Capys

A LAY SUNG AT THE BANQUET IN THE
CAPITOL, ON THE DAY WHEREON MANIUS
CURIUS DENTATUS, A SECOND TIME CONSUL,
TRIUMPHED OVER KING PYRRHUS AND THE
TARENTINES, IN THE YEAR OF THE CITY
CCCCLXXIX

1

Now slain is King Amulius,
    Of the great Sylvian line,
Who reigned in Alba Longa,
    On the throne of Aventine.
Slain is the Pontiff Camers,
    Who spake the words of doom:
'The children to the Tiber,
    The mother to the tomb.'

2

In Alba's lake no fisher
    His net today is flinging:
On the dark rind of Alba's oaks
    Today no axe is ringing:
The yoke hangs o'er the manger:
    The scythe lies in the hay:
Through all the Alban villages
    No work is done today

3

And every Alban burgher
    Hath donned his whitest gown;
And every head in Alba
    Weareth a poplar crown;
And every Alban door-post
    With boughs and flowers is gay,

For today the dead are living;
   The lost are found today.

4

They were doomed by a bloody king:
   They were doomed by a lying priest:
They were cast on the raging flood:
   They were tracked by the raging beast:
Raging beast and raging flood
   Alike have spared the prey;
And today the dead are living:
   The lost are found today.

5

The troubled river knew them,
   And smoothed his yellow foam
And gently rocked the cradle
   That bore the fate of Rome.
The ravening she-wolf knew them,
   And licked them o'er and o'er,
And gave them of her own fierce milk,
   Rich with raw flesh and gore.
Twenty winters, twenty springs,
   Since then have rolled away;
And today the dead are living:
   The lost are found today.

6

Blithe it was to see the twins,
   Right goodly youths and tall,
Marching from Alba Longa
   To their old grandsire's hall.
Along their path fresh garlands
   Are hung from tree to tree:
Before them stride the pipers,
   Piping a note of glee.

7

On the right goes Romulus,
  With arms to the elbows red,
And in his hand a broadsword,
  And on the blade a head –
A head in an iron helmet,
  With horse-hair hanging down
A shaggy head, a swarthy head,
  Fixed in a ghastly frown –
The head of King Amulius
  Of the great Sylvian line,
Who reigned in Alba Longa,
  On the throne of Aventine.

8

On the left side goes Remus,
  With wrists and fingers red,
And in his hand a boar-spear,
  And on the point a head –
A wrinkled head and aged,
  With silver beard and hair,
And holy fillets round it,
  Such as the pontiffs wear –
The head of ancient Camers,
  Who spake the words of doom:
'The children to the Tiber;
  The mother to the tomb.'

9

Two and two behind the twins
  Their trusty comrades go,
Four and forty valiant men,
  With club, and axe, and bow.
On each side every hamlet
  Pours forth its joyous crowd,
Shouting lads and baying dogs,
  And children laughing loud,

And old men weeping fondly
    As Rhea's boys go by,
And maids who shriek to see the heads,
    Yet, shrieking, press more nigh.

10

So they marched along the lake,
    They marched by fold and stall,
By cornfield and by vineyard,
    Unto the old man's hall.

11

In the hall-gate sat Capys,
    Capys, the sightless seer;
From head to foot he trembled
    As Romulus drew near.
And up stood stiff his thin white hair,
    And his blind eyes flashed fire:
'Hail! foster child of the wonderous nurse!
    Hail! son of the wonderous sire!

12

'But thou – what dost thou here
    In the old man's peaceful hall?
What doth the eagle in the coop,
    The bison in the stall?
Our corn fills many a garner;
    Our vines clasp many a tree;
Our flocks are white on many a hill,
    But these are not for thee.

13

'For thee no treasure ripens
    In the Tartessian mine:
For thee no ship brings precious bales
    Across the Libyan brine;
Thou shalt not drink from amber;
    Thou shalt not rest on down;

Arabia shall not steep thy locks,
   Nor Sidon tinge thy gown.

14

'Leave gold and myrrh and jewels,
   Rich table and soft bed,
To them who of man's seed are born,
   Whom woman's milk have fed.
Thou wast not made for lucre,
   For pleasure, nor for rest;
Thou, that art sprung from the War-god's loins,
   And hast tugged at the she-wolf's breast.

15

'From sunrise unto sunset
   All earth shall hear thy fame:
A glorious city thou shalt build,
   And name it by thy name:
And there, unquenched through ages,
   Like Vesta's sacred fire,
Shall live the spirit of thy nurse,
   The spirit of thy sire.

16

'The ox toils through the furrow,
   Obedient to the goad;
The patient ass, up flinty paths,
   Plods with his weary load:
With whine and bound the spaniel
   His master's whistle hears;
And the sheep yields her patiently
   To the loud clashing shears.

17

'But thy nurse will hear no master,
   Thy nurse will bear no load;
And woe to them that shear her,
   And woe to them that goad!

When all the pack, loud baying,
　　Her bloody lair surrounds,
She dies in silence, biting hard,
　　Amidst the dying hounds.

18

'Pomona loves the orchard;
　　And Liber loves the vine;
And Pales loves the straw-built shed
　　Warm with the breath of kine;
And Venus loves the whispers
　　Of plighted youth and maid,
In April's ivory moonlight
　　Beneath the chestnut shade.

19

'But thy father loves the clashing
　　Of broadsword and of shield:
He loves to drink the steam that reeks
　　From the fresh battle-field:
He smiles a smile more dreadful
　　Than his own dreadful frown,
When he sees the thick black cloud of smoke
　　Go up from the conquered town.

20

'And such as is the War-god,
　　The author of thy line,
And such as she who suckled thee,
　　Even such be thou and thine.
Leave to the soft Campanian
　　His baths and his perfumes;
Leave to the sordid race of Tyre
　　Their dyeing-vats and looms:
Leave to the sons of Carthage
　　The rudder and the oar:
Leave to the Greek his marble Nymphs
　　And scrolls of wordy lore.

21

'Thine, Roman, is the pilum:
　　Roman, the sword is thine,
The even trench, the bristling mound,
　　The legion's ordered line;
And thine the wheels of triumph,
　　Which with their laurelled train
Move slowly up the shouting streets
　　To Jove's eternal fane.

22

'Beneath thy yoke the Volscian
　　Shall vail his lofty brow:
Soft Capua's curled revellers
　　Before thy chairs shall bow:
The Lucumoes of Arnus
　　Shall quake thy rods to see;
And the proud Samnite's heart of steel
　　Shall yield to only thee.

23

'The Gaul shall come against thee
　　From the land of snow and night:
Thou shalt give his fair-haired armies
　　To the raven and the kite.

24

'The Greek shall come against thee,
　　The conqueror of the East.
Beside him stalks to battle
　　The hugh earth-shaking beast,
The beast on whom the castle
　　With all its guards doth stand,
The beast who hath between his eyes
　　The serpent for a hand.
First march the bold Epirotes,
　　Wedged close with shield and spear,

And the ranks of false Tarentum
   Are glittering in the rear.

25

'The ranks of false Tarentum
   Like hunted sheep shall fly:
In vain the bold Epirotes
   Shall round their standards die:
And Apennine's grey vultures
   Shall have a noble feast
On the fat and the eyes
   Of the huge earth-shaking beast.

26

'Hurrah! for the good weapons
   That keep the War-god's land.
Hurrah! for Rome's stout pilum
   In a stout Roman hand.
Hurrah! for Rome's short broadsword
   That through the thick array
Of levelled spears and serried shields
   Hews deep its gory way.

27

'Hurrah! for the great triumph
   That stretches many a mile.
Hurrah! for the wan captives
   That pass in endless file.
Ho! bold Epirotes, whither
   Hath the Red King ta'en flight?
Ho! dogs of false Tarentum,
   Is not the gown washed white?

28

'Hurrah! for the great triumph
   That stretches many a mile.
Hurrah! for the rich dye of Tyre,
   And the fine web of Nile,

The helmets gay with plumage
   Torn from the pheasants's wings,
The belts set thick with starry gems
   That shone on Indian kings,
The urns of massy silver,
   The goblets rough with gold,
The many-coloured tablets bright
   With loves and wars of old,
The stone that breathes and struggles,
   The brass that seems to speak; –
Such cunning they who dwell on high
   Have given unto the Greek.

29

'Hurrah! for Manius Curius,
   The bravest son of Rome,
Thrice in utmost need sent forth,
   Thrice drawn in triumph home.
Weave, weave, for Manius Curius
   The third embroidered gown:
Make ready the third lofty car,
   And twine the third green crown;
And yoke the steeds of Rosea
   With necks like a bended bow
And deck the bull, Mevania's bull,
   The bull as white as snow.

30

'Blest and thrice blest the Roman
   Who sees Rome's brightest day,
Who sees that long victorious pomp
   Wind down the Sacred Way,
And through the bellowing Forum,
   And round the Suppliant's Grove,
Up to the everlasting gates
   Of Capitolian Jove.

31

Then where, o'er two bright havens,
  The towers of Corinth frown;
Where the gigantic King of Day
  On his own Rhodes looks down;
Where soft Orontes murmurs
  Beneath the laurel shades;
Where Nile reflects the endless length
  Of dark red colonnades;
Where in the still deep water,
  Sheltered from waves and blasts,
Bristles the dusky forest
  Of Byrsa's thousand masts;
Where fur-clad hunters wander
  Amidst the northern ice;
Where through the sand of morning-land
  The camel bears the spice;
Where Atlas flings his shadow
  Far o'er the western foam,
Shall be great fear on all who hear
  The mighty name of Rome.'

MISCELLANEOUS POEMS

Lines to the Memory of Pitt

Oh Britain! dear Isle, when the annals of story
   Shall tell of the deeds that thy children have done,
When the strains of each poet shall sing of their glory,
   And the triumphs their skill and their valour have won;

When the olive and palm in thy chaplet are blended,
   When thy arts, and thy fame, and thy commerce increase,
When thy arms through the uttermost coasts are extended,
   And thy war is triumphant, and happy thy peace;

When the ocean, whose waves like a rampart flow round
     thee,
   Conveying thy mandates to every shore,
And the empire of nature no longer can bound thee,
   And the world be the scene of thy conquests no more:

Remember the man who in sorrow and danger,
   When thy glory was set, and thy spirit was low,
When thy hopes were o'erturned by the arms of the stranger,
   And thy banners displayed in the halls of the foe,

Stood forth in the tempest of doubt and disaster,
   Unaided, and single, the danger to brave,
Asserted thy claims, and the rights of his master,
   Preserved thee to conquer, and saved thee to save.

1813

A Radical War Song

Awake, arise, the hour is come,
　　For rows and revolutions;
There's no receipt like pike and drum
　　For crazy constitutions.
Close, close the shop! Break, break the loom,
　　Desert your hearths and furrows,
And throng in arms to seal the doom
　　Of England's rotten boroughs.

We'll stretch that tort'ring Castlereagh
　　On his own Dublin rack, sir;
We'll drown the King in Eau de vie,
　　The Laureate in his sack, sir.
Old Eldon and his sordid hag
　　In molten gold we'll smother,
And stifle in his own green bag
　　The Doctor and his brother.

In chains we'll hang in fair Guildhall
　　The City's famed Recorder,
And next on proud St Stephen's fall,
　　Though Wynne should squeak to order.
In vain our tyrants then shall try
　　To 'scape our martial law, sir;
In vain the trembling Speaker cry
　　That "Strangers must withdraw," sir.

Copley to hang offends no text;
　　A rat is not a man, sir:
With schedules and with tax bills next
　　We'll bury pious Van, sir.
The slaves who loved the Income Tax,
　　We'll crush by scores, like mites, sir,
And him, the wretch who freed the blacks,
　　And more enslaved the whites, sir.

The peer shall dangle from his gate,
    The bishop from his steeple,
Till all recanting, own, the State
    Means nothing but the People.
We'll fix the church's revenues
    On Apostolic basis,
One coat, one scrip, one pair of shoes
    Shall pay their strange grimaces.

We'll strap the bar's deluding train
    In their own darling halter,
And with his big church bible brain
    The parson at the altar.
Hail glorious hour, when fair Reform
    Shall bless our longing nation,
And Hunt receive commands to form
    A new administration.

Carlisle shall sit enthroned, where sat
    Our Cranmer and our Secker;
And Watson show his snow-white hat
    In England's rich Exchequer.
The breast of Thistlewood shall wear
    Our Wellesley's star and sash, man;
And many a mausoleum fair
    Shall rise to honest Cashman.

Then, then beneath the nine-tailed cat
    Shall they who used it writhe, sir;
And curates lean, and rectors fat,
    Shall dig the ground they tithe, sir.
Down with your Bayleys, and your Bests,
    Your Giffords, and your Gurneys:
We'll clear the island of the pests,
    Which mortals name attorneys.

Down with your sheriffs, and your mayors,
    Your registrars, and proctors,
We'll live without the lawyer's cares,
    And die without the doctor's.

No discontented fair shall pout
    To see her spouse so stupid;
We'll tread the torch of Hymen out,
    And live content with Cupid.

Then, when the high-born and the great
    Are humbled to our level,
On all the wealth of Church and State,
    Like aldermen, we'll revel.
We'll live when hushed the battle's din,
    In smoking and in cards, sir,
In drinking unexcised gin,
    And wooing fair Poissardes, sir.

1820

Epitaph on Henry Martyn

Here Martyn lies. In Manhood's early bloom
The Christian Hero finds a Pagan tomb.
Religion, sorrowing o'er her favourite son,
Points to the glorious trophies that he won.
Eternal trophies! not with carnage red,
Not stained with tears by hapless captives shed,
But trophies of the Cross! for that dear name,
Through every form of danger, death and shame,
Onward he journeyed to a happier shore,
Where danger, death and shame assault no more.

1812

Ivry

A SONG OF THE HUGUENOTS

Now glory to the Lord of Hosts, from whom all glories are!
And glory to our Sovereign Liege, King Henry of Navarre!
Now let there be the merry sound of music and of dance,
Through thy corn-fields green, and sunny vines, oh pleasant
    land of France!
And thou, Rochelle, our own Rochelle, proud city of the
    waters,
Again let rapture light the eyes of all thy mourning
    daughters.
As thou wert constant in our ills, be joyous in our joy,
For cold, and stiff, and still are they who wrought thy walls
    annoy.
Hurrah! Hurrah! a single field hath turned the chance of
    war,
Hurrah! Hurrah! for Ivry, and Henry of Navarre.

Oh! how our hearts were beating, when, at the dawn of day,
We saw the army of the League drawn out in long array;
With all its priest-led citizens, and all its rebel peers,
And Appenzel's stout infantry, and Egmont's Flemish
    spears.
There rode the brood of false Lorraine, the curses of our
    land;
And dark Mayenne was in the midst, a truncheon in his
    hand:
And, as we looked on them, we thought of Seine's
    empurpled flood,
And good Coligni's hoary hair all dabbled with his blood;
And we cried unto the living God, who rules the fate of war,
To fight for his own holy name, and Henry of Navarre.

The King is come to marshal us, in all his armour drest,
And he has bound a snow-white plume upon his gallant
    crest.

He looked upon his people, and a tear was in his eye;
He looked upon the traitors, and his glance was stern and
     high.
Right graciously he smiled on us, as rolled from wing to wing,
Down all our line, a deafening shout, 'God save our Lord the
     King!'
'An if my standard-bearer fall, as fall full well he may,
For never saw I promise yet of such a bloody fray,
Press where ye see my white plume shine, amidst the ranks of
     war,
And be your oriflamme today the helmet of Navarre.'

Hurrah! the foes are moving. Hark to the mingled din,
Of fife, and steed, and trump, and drum, and roaring
     culverin.
The fiery Duke is pricking fast across Saint André's plain,
With all the hireling chivalry of Guelders and Almayne.
Now by the lips of those ye love, fair gentlemen of France,
Charge for the golden lilies, – upon them with the lance.
A thousand spurs are striking deep, a thousand spears in rest,
A thousand knights are pressing close behind the snow-white
     crest;
And in they burst, and on they rushed, while, like a guiding
     star,
Amidst the thickest carnage blazed the helmet of Navarre.

Now, God be praised, the day is ours. Mayenne hath turned
     his rein.
D'Aumale hath cried for quarter. The Flemish count is slain.
Their ranks are breaking like thin clouds before a Biscay gale;
The field is heaped with bleeding steeds, and flags, and cloven
     mail.
And then we thought on vengeance, and, all along our van,
'Remember Saint Bartholomew,' was passed from man to
     man.
But out spake gentle Henry, 'No Frenchman is my foe:
Down, down, with every foreigner, but let your brethren go.'
Oh! was there ever such a knight, in friendship or in war,
As our Sovereign Lord, King Henry, the soldier of Navarre?

Right well fought all the Frenchmen who fought for France
    today;
And many a lordly banner God gave them for a prey.
But we of the religion have borne us best in fight;
And the good Lord of Rosny hath ta'en the cornet white.
Our own true Maximilian the cornet white hath ta'en,
The cornet white with crosses black, the flag of false
    Lorraine.
Up with it high; unfurl it wide; that all the host may know
How God hath humbled the proud house which wrought his
    church such woe.
Then on the ground, while trumpets sound their loudest
    point of war,
Fling the red shreds, a footcloth meet for Henry of Navarre.

Ho! maidens of Vienna; Ho! matrons of Lucerne;
Weep, weep, and rend your hair for those who never shall
    return.
Ho! Philip, send, for charity, thy Mexican pistoles,
That Antwerp monks may sing a mass for thy poor
    spearmen's souls.
Ho! gallant nobles of the League, look that your arms be
    bright;
Ho! burghers of Saint Genevieve, keep watch and ward
    tonight.
For our God hath crushed the tyrant, our God hath raised
    the slave,
And mocked the counsel of the wise, and the valour of the
    brave,
Then glory to his holy name, from whom all glories are;
And glory to our Sovereign Lord, King Henry of Navarre.

1824

The Battle of Moncontour

Oh, weep for Moncontour! Oh! weep for the hour
When the children of darkness and evil had power,
When the horsemen of Valois triumphantly trod
On the bosoms that bled for their rights and their God.

Oh, weep for Moncontour! Oh! weep for the slain,
Who for faith and for freedom lay slaughtered in vain;
Oh, weep for the living, who linger to bear
The renegade's shame, or the exile's despair.

One look, one last look, to our cots and our towers,
To the rows of our vines, and the beds of our flowers,
To the church where the bones of our fathers decayed,
Where we fondly had deemed that our own would be laid.

Alas! we must leave thee, dear desolate home,
To the spearmen of Uri, the shavelings of Rome,
To the serpent of Florence, the vulture of Spain,
To the pride of Anjou, and the guile of Lorraine.

Farewell to thy fountains, farewell to thy shades,
To the song of thy youths, and the dance of thy maids,
To the breath of thy gardens, the hum of thy bees,
And the long waving line of the blue Pyrenees.

Farewell, and for ever. The priest and the slave
May rule in the halls of the free and the brave.
Our hearths we abandon; our lands we resign;
But, Father, we kneel to no altar but thine.

1824

Songs of the Civil War – 1

THE BATTLE OF NASEBY, BY OBADIAH
BIND-THEIR-KINGS-IN-CHAINS-AND-
THEIR-NOBLES-WITH-LINKS-OF-IRON,
SERJEANT IN IRETON'S REGIMENT

Oh! wherefore come ye forth, in triumph from the North,
    With your hands, and your feet, and your raiment all red?
And wherefore doth your rout send forth a joyous shout?
    And whence be the grapes of the wine-press which ye
        tread?

Oh evil was the root, and bitter was the fruit,
    And crimson was the juice of the vintage that we trod;
For we trampled on the throng of the haughty and the
        strong,
    Who sat in the high places, and slew the saints of God.

It was about the noon of a glorious day of June,
    That we saw their banners dance, and their cuirasses
        shine,
And the Man of Blood was there, with his long essenced hair,
    And Astley, and Sir Marmaduke, and Rupert of the Rhine.

Like a servant of the Lord, with his Bible and his sword,
    The General rode along us to form us to the fight,
When a murmuring sound broke out, and swell'd into a
        shout,
    Among the godless horsemen upon the tyrant's right.

And hark! like the roar of the billows on the shore,
    The cry of battle rises along their charging line!
For God! for the Cause! for the Church, for the Laws!
    For Charles King of England, and Rupert of the Rhine!

The furious German comes, with his clarions and his drums,
    His bravoes of Alsatia, and pages of Whitehall;
They are bursting on our flanks. Grasp your pikes, close your
        ranks;
    For Rupert never comes but to conquer or to fall.

They are here! They rush on! We are broken! We are gone!
    Our left is borne before them like stubble on the blast.
O Lord, put forth thy might! O Lord, defend the right!
    Stand back to back, in God's name, and fight it to the last.

Stout Skippon hath a wound; the centre hath given ground:
    Hark! hark! – What means the trampling of horsemen on
        our rear?
Whose banner do I see, boys? 'Tis he, thank God, 'tis he,
        boys.
    Bear up another minute: brave Oliver is here.

Their heads all stooping low, their points all in a row,
    Like a whirlwind on the trees, like a deluge on the dykes,
Our cuirassiers have burst on the ranks of the Accurst,
    And at a shock have scattered the forest of his pikes.

Fast, fast, the gallants ride, in some safe nook to hide
    Their coward heads, predestined to rot on Temple Bar:
And he – he turns, he flies: – shame on those cruel eyes
    That bore to look on torture, and dare not look on war.

Ho! comrades, scour the plain; and, ere ye strip the slain,
    First give another stab to make your search secure,
Then shake from sleeves and pockets their broadpieces and
        lockets,
    The tokens of the wanton, the plunder of the poor.

Fools! your doublets shone with gold, and your hearts were
        gay and bold,
    When you kissed your lily hands to your lemans today;
And tomorrow shall the fox, from her chambers in the rocks,
    Lead forth her tawny cubs to howl above the prey.

Where be your tongues that late mocked at heaven and hell
    and fate,
  And the fingers that once were so busy with your blades,
Your perfum'd satin clothes, your catches and your oaths,
  Your stage-plays and your sonnets, your diamonds and
    your spades?

Down, down, for ever down with the mitre and the crown,
  With the Belial of the Court, and the Mammon of the
    Pope;
There is woe in Oxford Halls; there is wail in Durham's
    Stalls:
  The Jesuit smites his bosom: the Bishop rends his cope.

And She of the seven hills shall mourn her children's ills,
  And tremble when she thinks on the edge of England's
    sword;
And the Kings of earth in fear shall shudder when they hear
  What the hand of God hath wrought for the Houses and
    the Word.

                              1824

Songs of the Civil War – 2

Here warlike coblers railed from tops of casks
At lords and love-locks, monarchy and masques.
There many a graceless page blaspheming reel'd,
From his dear cards and bumpers, to the field:
The famished rooks, impatient of delay,
Gnaw their cogg'd dice and curse the lingering prey:
His sad Andromache, with fruitless care,
Paints her wan lips and braids her borrowed hair:
For Church and King he quits his favourite arts,
Forsakes his Knaves, forsakes his Queen of Hearts:
For Church and King he burns to stain with gore
His doublet, stained with nought but sack before.

from a MS Poem

THE CAVALIER'S MARCH TO LONDON

To horse! to horse! brave Cavaliers!
    To horse for Church and Crown!
Strike, strike your tents! snatch up your spears!
    And ho for London town!
The imperial harlot, doom'd a prey
    To our avenging fires,
Sends up the voice of her dismay
    From all her hundred spires.

The Strand resounds with maidens' shrieks,
    The 'Change with merchants' sighs,
And blushes stand on brazen cheeks,
    And tears in iron eyes;
And, pale with fasting and with fright,
    Each Puritan Committee
Hath summon'd forth to prayer and fight
    The Roundheads of the City.

And soon shall London's sentries hear
   The thunder of our drum,
And London's dames, in wilder fear,
   Shall cry, Alack! They come!
Fling the fascines; – tear up the spikes;
   And forward, one and all.
Down, down with all their train-band pikes,
   Down with their mud-built wall.

Quarter? – Foul fall your whining noise,
   Ye recreant spawn of fraud!
No quarter! Think on Strafford, boys.
   No quarter! Think on Laud.
What ho! The craven slaves retire.
   On! Trample them to mud,
No quarter! – Charge. – No quarter! – Fire.
   No quarter! – Blood! – Blood! – Blood! –

Where next? In sooth there lacks no witch,
   Brave lads, to tell us where,
Sure London's sons be passing rich,
   Her daughters wondrous fair:
And let that dastard be the theme
   Of many a board's derision,
Who quails for sermon, cuff, or scream
   Of any sweet Precisian.

Their lean divines, of solemn brow,
   Sworn foes to throne and steeple,
From an unwonted pulpit now
   Shall edify the people:
Till the tir'd hangman, in despair,
   Shall curse his blunted shears,
And vainly pinch, and scrape, and tear,
   Around their leathern ears.

We'll hang, above his own Guildhall,
   The city's grave Recorder,
And on the den of thieves we'll fall,
   Though Pym should speak to order.

In vain the lank-haired gang shall try
   To cheat our martial law;
In vain shall Lenthall trembling cry
   That strangers must withdraw.

Of bench and woolsack, tub and chair,
   We'll build a glorious pyre,
And tons of rebel parchment there
   Shall crackle in the fire.
With them shall perish, cheek by jowl,
   Petition, psalm, and libel,
The Colonel's canting muster-roll,
   The Chaplain's dog-ear'd bible.

We'll tread a measure round the blaze
   Where England's pest expires,
And lead along the dance's maze
   The beauties of the friars:
Then smiles in every face shall shine,
   And joy in every soul.
Bring forth, bring forth the oldest wine,
   And crown the largest bowl.

And as with nod and laugh ye sip
   The goblet's rich carnation,
Whose bursting bubbles seem to tip
   The wink of invitation;
Drink to those names, – those glorious names, –
   Those names no time shall sever, –
Drink, in a draught as deep as Thames,
   Our Church and King for ever!

                        1824

Sermon in a Churchyard

Let pious Damon take his seat,
   With mincing step, and languid smile,
And scatter from his 'kerchief sweet,
   Sabæan odours o'er the aisle;
And spread his little jewelled hand,
   And smile round all the parish beauties,
And pat his curls, and smooth his band,
   Meet prelude to his saintly duties.

Let the thronged audience press and stare,
   Let stifled maidens ply the fan,
Admire his doctrines and his hair,
   And whisper 'What a good young man!'
While he explains what seems most clear,
   So clearly that it seems perplexed,
I'll stay, and read my sermon here;
   And skulls, and bones, shall be the text.

Art thou the jilted dupe of fame?
   Dost thou with jealous anger pine
Whene'er she sounds some other name,
   With fonder emphasis than thine?
To thee I preach; draw near; attend!
   Look on these bones, thou fool, and see
Where all her scorns and favours end,
   What Byron is, and thou must be.

Dost thou revere, or praise, or trust
   Some clod like those that here we spurn;
Some thing that sprang like thee from dust,
   And shall like thee to dust return?
Dost thou rate statesmen, heroes, wits,
   At one sear leaf or wandering feather?
Behold the black, damp, narrow pits,
   Where they and thou must lie together.

Dost thou beneath the smile or frown
   Of some vain woman bend thy knee?
Here take thy stand, and trample down
   Things that were once as fair as she.
Here rave of her ten thousand graces,
   Bosom, and lip, and eye, and chin,
While, as in scorn, the fleshless faces
   Of Hamiltons and Waldegraves grin.

Whate'er thy losses or thy gains,
   Whate'er thy projects or thy fears,
Whate'er the joys, whate'er the pains,
   That prompt thy baby smiles and tears,
Come to my school, and thou shalt learn,
   In one short hour of placid thought,
A stoicism, more deep, more stern,
   Than ever Zeno's porch hath taught.

The plots and feats of those that press
   To seize on titles, wealth, or power,
Shall seem to thee a game of chess,
   Devised to pass a tedious hour.
What matters it to him who fights
   For shows of unsubstantial good,
Whether his Kings, and Queens, and Knights,
   Be things of flesh, or things of wood?

We check, and take; exult and fret;
   Our plans extend, our passions rise,
Till in our ardour we forget
   How worthless is the victor's prize.
Soon fades the spell, soon comes the night:
   Say will it not be then the same,
Whether we played the black or white,
   Whether we lost or won the game?

Dost thou among these hillocks stray,
   O'er some dear idol's tomb to moan?
Know that thy foot is on the clay
   Of hearts once wretched as thy own.

How many a father's anxious schemes,
　　How many rapturous thoughts of lovers,
How many a mother's cherished dreams,
　　The swelling turf before thee covers!

Here for the living, and the dead,
　　The weepers and the friends they weep,
Hath been ordained the same cold bed,
　　The same dark night, the same long sleep.
Why shouldest thou writhe, and sob, and rave
　　O'er those, with whom thou soon must be?
Death his own sting shall cure – the grave
　　Shall vanquish its own victory.

Here learn that all the griefs and joys,
　　Which now torment, which now beguile,
Are children's hurts, and children's toys,
　　Scarce worthy of one bitter smile.
Here learn that pulpit, throne, and press,
　　Sword, sceptre, lyre, alike are frail,
That science is a blind man's guess,
　　And History a nurse's tale.

Here learn that glory and disgrace,
　　Wisdom and folly, pass away,
That mirth hath its appointed space,
　　That sorrow is but for a day;
That all we love, and all we hate,
　　That all we hope, and all we fear,
Each mood of mind, each turn of fate,
　　Must end in dust and silence here.

1825

Dies Irae

On that great, that awful day,
This vain world shall pass away.
Thus the sibyl sang of old,
Thus hath Holy David told.
There shall be a deadly fear
When the Avenger shall appear,
And unveiled before his eye
All the works of man shall lie.
Hark! to the great trumpet's tones
Pealing o'er the place of bones:
Hark! it waketh from their bed
All the nations of the dead, –
In a countless throng to meet,
At the eternal judgment seat.
Nature sickens with dismay,
Death may not retain his prey;
And before the Maker stand
All the creatures of his hand.
The great book shall be unfurled,
Whereby God shall judge the world:
What was distant shall be near,
What was hidden shall be clear.
To what shelter shall I fly?
To what guardian shall I cry?
Oh, in that destroying hour,
Source of goodness, Source of power,
Show thou, of thine own free grace,
Help unto a helpless race.
Though I plead not at thy throne
Aught that I for thee have done,
Do not thou unmindful be,
Of what thou hast borne for me:
Of the wandering, of the scorn,
Of the scourge, and of the thorn.
Jesus, hast *thou* borne the pain,

And hath all been borne in vain?
Shall thy vengeance smite the head
For whose ransom thou hast bled?
Thou, whose dying blessing gave
Glory to a guilty slave:
Thou, who from the crew unclean
Did'st release the Magdalene:
Shall not mercy vast and free,
Evermore be found in thee?
Father, turn on me thine eyes,
See my blushes, hear my cries;
Faint though be the cries I make,
Save me, for thy mercy's sake,
From the worm, and from the fire,
From the torments of thine ire.
Fold me with the sheep that stand
Pure and safe at thy right hand.
Hear thy guilty child implore thee,
Rolling in the dust before thee.
Oh the horrors of that day!
When this frame of sinful clay,
Starting from its burial place,
Must behold thee face to face.
Hear and pity, hear and aid,
Spare the creatures thou hast made.
Mercy, mercy, save, forgive,
Oh, who shall look on thee and live?

1826

The Marriage of Tirzah and Ahirad

GENESIS VI. 3

It is the dead of night:
Yet more than noonday light
Beams far and wide from many a gorgeous hall.
Unnumbered harps are tinkling,
Unnumbered lamps are twinkling,
In the great city of the fourfold wall.
By the brazen castle's moat,
The sentry hums a livelier note.
The ship-boy chaunts a shriller lay
From the galleys in the bay.
Shout, and laugh, and hurrying feet
Sound from mart and square and street,
From the breezy laurel shades,
From the granite colonnades,
From the golden statue's base,
From the stately market-place,
Where, upreared by captive hands,
The great Tower of Triumph stands,
All its pillars in a blaze
With the many-coloured rays,
Which lanthorns of ten thousand dyes
Shed on ten thousand panoplies.
But closest is the throng,
And loudest is the song,
In that sweet garden by the river's side,
The abyss of myrtle bowers,
The wilderness of flowers,
Where Cain hath built the palace of his pride.
Such palace ne'er shall be again
Among the dwindling race of men.
From all its threescore gates the light
Of gold and steel afar was thrown;
Two hundred cubits rose in height

The outer wall of polished stone.
On the top was ample space
For a gallant chariot race.
Near either parapet a bed
Of the richest mould was spread,
Where amidst flowers of every scent and hue
Rich orange trees, and palms, and giant cedars grew.

In the mansion's public court
All is revel, song, and sport;
For there, till morn shall tint the east,
Menials and guards prolong the feast.
The boards with painted vessels shine;
The marble cisterns foam with wine.
A hundred dancing girls are there
With zoneless waists and streaming hair;
And countless eyes with ardour gaze,
And countless hands the measure beat,
As mix and part in amorous maze
Those floating arms and bounding feet.
But none of all the race of Cain,
Save those whom he hath deigned to grace
With yellow robe and sapphire chain,
May pass beyond that outer space.
For now within the painted hall
The Firstborn keeps high festival.
Before the glittering valves all night
Their post the chosen captains hold,
Above the portal's stately height
The legend flames in lamps of gold:
'In life united and in death
May Tirzah and Ahirad be,
The bravest he of all the sons of Seth,
Of all the house of Cain the loveliest she.'

Through all the climates of the earth
This night is given to festal mirth.
The long continued war is ended.
The long divided lines are blended.
Ahirad's bow shall now no more

Make fat the wolves with kindred gore.
The vultures shall expect in vain
Their banquet from the sword of Cain.
Without a guard the herds and flocks
Along the frontier moors and rocks
    From eve to morn may roam;
Nor shriek, nor shout, nor reddened sky,
Shall warn the startled hind to fly
    From his beloved home.
Nor to the pier shall burghers crowd
    With straining necks and faces pale,
And think that in each flitting cloud
    They see a hostile sail.
The peasant without fear shall guide
Down smooth canal or river wide
    His painted bark of cane,
Fraught, for some proud bazaar's arcades,
With chestnuts from his native shades,
    And wine, and milk, and grain.
Search round the peopled globe tonight,
    Explore each continent and isle,
There is no door without a light,
    No face without a smile.
The noblest chiefs of either race,
    From north and south, from west and east,
Crowd to the painted hall to grace
    The pomp of that atoning feast.
With widening eyes and labouring breath
Stand the fair-haired sons of Seth,
As bursts upon their dazzled sight
The endless avenue of light,
The bowers of tulip, rose, and palm,
The thousand cressets fed with balm,
The silken vests, the boards piled high
With amber, gold, and ivory,
The crystal founts whence sparkling flow
The richest wines o'er beds of snow,
The walls where blaze in living dyes
The king's three hundred victories.
The heralds point the fitting seat

To every guest in order meet,
And place the highest in degree
Nearest th' imperial canopy.
Beneath its broad and gorgeous fold,
With naked swords and shields of gold,
Stood the seven princes of the tribes of Nod.
Upon an ermine carpet lay
Two tiger cubs in furious play,
Beneath the emerald throne where sat the signed of God.

Over that ample forehead white
The thousandth year returneth.
Still, on its commanding height,
With a fierce and blood-red light,
The fiery token burneth.
Wheresoe'er that mystic star
Blazeth in the van of war,
Back recoil before its ray
Shield and banner, bow and spear,
Maddened horses break away
From the trembling charioteer.
The fear of that stern king doth lie
On all that live beneath the sky;
All shrink before the mark of his despair,
The seal of that great curse which he alone can bear.

Blazing in pearls and diamonds' sheen,
Tirzah, the young Ahirad's bride,
Of humankind the destined queen,
Sits by her great forefather's side.
The jetty curls, the forehead high,
The swanlike neck, the eagle face,
The glowing cheek, the rich dark eye,
Proclaim her of the elder race.
With flowing locks of auburn hue,
And features smooth, and eye of blue,
Timid in love as brave in arms,
The gentle heir of Seth askance
Snatches a bashful, ardent glance
At her majestic charms;

Blest when across that brow high musing flashes
    A deeper tint of rose,
Thrice blest when from beneath the silken lashes
    Of her proud eye she throws
The smile of blended fondness and disdain
Which marks the daughters of the house of Cain.

    All hearts are light around the hall
    Save his who is the lord of all.
    The painted roofs, the attendant train,
    The lights, the banquet, all are vain.
    He sees them not. His fancy strays
    To other scenes and other days.
    A cot by a lone forest's edge,
       A fountain murmuring through the trees,
    A garden with a wild flower hedge,
       Whence sounds the music of the bees,
    A little flock of sheep at rest
    Upon a mountain's swarthy breast.
    On his rude spade he seems to lean
       Beside the well remembered stone,
    Rejoicing o'er the promise green
       Of the first harvest man hath sown.
       He sees his mother's tears;
       His father's voice he hears,
Kind as when first it praised his youthful skill.
       And soon a seraph-child,
       In boyish rapture wild,
With a light crook comes bounding from the hill,
       Kisses his hands, and strokes his face,
       And nestles close in his embrace.
       In his adamantine eye
       None might discern his agony;
But they who had grown hoary next his side,
    And read his stern dark face with deepest skill,
Could trace strange meanings in that lip of pride,
    Which for one moment quivered and was still.
No time for them to mark or him to feel
    Those inward stings; for clarion, flute, and lyre
    And the rich voices of a countless quire,

Burst on the ear in one triumphant peal.
In breathless transport sits the admiring throng,
As sink and swell the notes of Jubal's lofty song.

'Sound the timbrel, strike the lyre,
Wake the trumpet's blast of fire,
   Till the gilded arches ring.
Empire, victory, and fame,
Be ascribed unto the name
   Of our father and our king.
Of the deeds which he hath done,
Of the spoils which he hath won,
   Let his grateful children sing.

'When the deadly fight was fought,
When the great revenge was wrought,
When on the slaughtered victims lay
The minion stiff and cold as they,
Doomed to exile, sealed with flame,
From the west the wanderer came.
Six score years and six he strayed
A hunter through the forest shade.
The lion's shaggy jaws he tore,
To earth he smote the foaming boar,
He crushed the dragon's fiery crest,
And scaled the condor's dizzy nest;
Till hardy sons and daughters fair
Increased around his woodland lair.
Then his victorious bow unstrung
On the great bison's horn he hung.
Giraffe and elk he left to hold
   The wilderness of boughs in peace,
And trained his youth to pen the fold,
   To press the cream, and weave the fleece.
As shrunk the streamlet in its bed,
   As black and scant the herbage grew,
O'er endless plains his flocks he led
   Still to new brooks and pastures new.
So strayed he till the white pavilions
Of his camp were told by millions,
Till his children's households seven

Were numerous as the stars of heaven.
Then he bade us rove no more;
   And in the place that pleased him best,
On the great river's fertile shore,
   He fixed the city of his rest.
He taught us then to bind the sheaves,
   To strain the palm's delicious milk,
And from the dark green mulberry leaves
   To cull the filmy silk.
Then first from straw-built mansions roamed
   O'er flower-beds trim the skilful bees;
Then first the purple wine vats foamed
   Around the laughing peasant's knees;
And olive-yards, and orchards green,
O'er all the hills of Nod were seen.

'Of our father and our king
Let his grateful children sing.
From him our race its being draws,
His are our arts, and his our laws.
Like himself he bade us be,
Proud, and brave, and fierce, and free.
True, through every turn of fate,
In our friendship and our hate.
Calm to watch, yet prompt to dare;
Quick to feel, yet firm to bear;
Only timid, only weak,
Before sweet woman's eye and cheek.
We will not serve, we will not know,
The God who is our father's foe.
In our proud cities to his name
No temples rise, no altars flame.
Our flocks of sheep, our groves of spice,
To him afford no sacrifice.
Enough that once the House of Cain
Hath courted with oblation vain
   The sullen power above.
Henceforth we bear the yoke no more;
The only gods whom we adore
   Are glory, vengeance, love.

'Of our father and our king
Let his grateful children sing.
What eye of living thing may brook
On his blazing brow to look?
What might of living thing may stand
Against the strength of his right hand?
First he led his armies forth
Against the Mammoths of the north,
What time they wasted in their pride
Pasture and vineyard far and wide.
Then the White River's icy flood
Was thawed with fire and dyed with blood.
And heard for many a league the sound
Of the pine forests blazing round,
And the death-howl and trampling din
Of the gigantic herd within.
From the surging sea of flame
Forth the tortured monsters came;
As of breakers on the shore
Was their onset and their roar;
As the cedar-trees of God
Stood the stately ranks of Nod.
One long night and one short day
The sword was lifted up to slay.
    Then marched the firstborn and his sons
O'er the white ashes of the wood,
And counted of that savage brood
    Nine times nine thousand skeletons.

'On the snow with carnage red
The wood is piled, the skins are spread.
A thousand fires illume the sky;
Round each a hundred warriors lie.
But, long ere half the night was spent,
Forth thundered from the golden tent
    The rousing voice of Cain.
A thousand trumps in answer rang,
And fast to arms the warriors sprang
    O'er all the frozen plain.
A herald from the wealthy bay

Hath come with tidings of dismay.
From the western ocean's coast
Seth hath led a countless host,
And vows to slay with fire and sword
All who call not on the Lord.
His archers hold the mountain forts;
His light armed ships blockade the ports;
    His horsemen tread the harvest down.
On twelve proud bridges he hath passed
The river dark with many a mast,
And pitched his mighty camp at last
    Before the imperial town.

'On the south and on the west,
Closely was the city prest.
Before us lay the hostile powers.
The breach was wide between the towers.
Pulse and meal within were sold
For a double weight of gold.
Our mighty father had gone forth
Two hundred marches to the north.
Yet in that extreme of ill
We stoutly kept his city still;
And swore beneath his royal wall,
Like his true sons, to fight and fall.

'Hark, hark, to gong and horn,
Clarion, and fife, and drum,
The morn, the fortieth morn,
Fixed for the great assault is come.
Between the camp and city spreads
A waving sea of helmed heads.
From the royal car of Seth
Was hung the blood-red flag of death:
At sight of that thrice-hallowed sign
Wide flew at once each banner's fold;
The captains clashed their arms of gold,
The war cry of Elohim rolled
Far down their endless line.
On the northern hills afar

Pealed an answering note of war.
Soon the dust in whirlwinds driven,
Rushed across the northern heaven.
Beneath its shroud came thick and loud
The tramp as of a countless crowd;
And at intervals were seen
Lance and hauberk glancing sheen;
And at intervals were heard
Charger's neigh and battle word.

'Oh what a rapturous cry
From all the city's thousand spires arose,
With what a look the hollow eye
Of the lean watchman glared upon the foes,
With what a yell of joy the mother pressed
The moaning baby to her withered breast,
When through the swarthy cloud that veiled the plain
Burst on his children's sight the flaming brow of Cain!'

There paused perforce that noble song;
For from all the joyous throng,
Burst forth a rapturous shout which drowned
Singer's voice and trumpet's sound.
Thrice that stormy clamour fell,
Thrice rose again with mightier swell.
The last and loudest roar of all
Had died along the painted wall.
The crowd was hushed; the minstrel train
Prepared to strike the chords again;
When on each ear distinctly smote
A low and wild and wailing note.
It moans again. In mute amaze
Menials, and guests, and harpers gaze.
They look above, beneath, around,
No shape doth own that mournful sound.
It comes not from the tuneful quire;
    It comes not from the feasting peers;
There is no tone of earthly lyre
    So soft, so sad, so full of tears.
Then a strange horror came on all

Who sat at that high festival.
The far famed harp, the harp of gold,
Dropped from Jubal's trembling hold.
Frantic with dismay the bride
Clung to her Ahirad's side.
And the corpse-like hue of dread
Ahirad's haughty face o'erspread.
Yet not even in that agony of awe
Did the young leader of the fair-haired race
From Tirzah's shuddering grasp his hand withdraw
Or turn his eyes from Tirzah's livid face.
The tigers to their lord retreat,
And crouch and whine beneath his feet.
Prone sink to earth the golden shielded seven.
All hearts are cowed save his alone
Who sits upon the emerald throne;
For he hath heard Elohim speak from heaven.
Still thunders in his ear the peal;
Still blazes on his front the seal:
And on the soul of the proud king
No terror of created thing
From sky, or earth, or hell, hath power
Since that unutterable hour.

He rose to speak, but paused, and listening stood,
Not daunted, but in sad and curious mood,
With knitted brow, and searching eye of fire.
A deathlike silence sank on all around,
And through the boundless space was heard no
    sound,
Save the soft tones of that mysterious lyre.
Broken, faint, and low,
At first the numbers flow.
Louder, deeper, quicker, still
Into one fierce peal they swell,
And the echoing palace fill
With a strange funereal yell.
A voice comes forth. But what, or where?
On the earth, or in the air?
Like the midnight winds that blow

Round a lone cottage in the snow,
With howling swell and sighing fall,
It wails along the trophied hall.
In such a wild and dreary moan
    The watches of the Seraphim
    Poured out all night their plaintive hymn
Before the eternal throne.
Then, when from many a heavenly eye
    Drops as of earthly pity fell
For her who had aspired too high,
    For him who loved too well.
When, stunned by grief, the gentle pair
From the nuptial garden fair,
Linked in a sorrowful caress,
Strayed through the untrodden wilderness:
And close behind their footsteps came
The desolating sword of flame,
And drooped the cedared alley's pride,
And fountains shrank, and roses died.

'Rejoice, oh Son of God, rejoice,'
Sang that melancholy voice,
'Rejoice, the maid is fair to see;
The bower is decked for her and thee;
The ivory lamps around it throw
A soft and pure and mellow glow.
Where'er the chastened lustre falls
On roof or cornice, floor or walls,
Woven of pink and rose appear
Such words as love delights to hear.
The breath of myrrh, the lute's soft sound,
Float through the moonlight galleries round.
O'er beds of violet and through groves of spice,
    Lead thy proud bride into the nuptial bower;
For thou hast bought her with a fearful price,
    And she hath dowered thee with a fearful
        dower.
The price is life. The dower is death.
    Accursed loss! Accursed gain!
For her thou givest the blessedness of Seth,

And to thine arms she brings the curse of Cain.
Round the dark curtains of the fiery throne
    Pauses awhile the voice of sacred song:
From all the angelic ranks goes forth a groan,
    "How long, O Lord, how long?"
The still small voice makes answer, "Wait and see,
Oh sons of glory, what the end shall be."

'But, in the outer darkness of the place
Where God hath shown his power without his grace,
    Is laughter and the sound of glad acclaim,
        Loud as when, on wings of fire,
        Fulfilled of his malign desire,
    From Paradise the conquering serpent came.
The giant ruler of the morning star
        From off his fiery bed
        Lifts high his stately head,
Which Michael's sword hath marked with many a scar.
        At his voice the pit of hell
        Answers with a joyous yell,
        And flings her dusky portals wide
        For the bridegroom and the bride.

        'But louder still shall be the din
        In the halls of Death and Sin,
        When the full measure runneth o'er,
        When mercy can endure no more,
        When he who vainly proffers grace,
        Comes in his fury to deface
            The fair creation of his hand;
        When from the heaven streams down amain
        For forty days the sheeted rain;
        And from his ancient barriers free,
        With a deafening roar the sea
            Comes foaming up the land.
        Mother, cast thy babe aside:
        Bridegroom, quit thy virgin bride:
        Brother, pass thy brother by:
        'Tis for life, for life, ye fly.
        Along the drear horizon raves

The swift advancing line of waves.
On: on: their frothy crests appear
Each moment nearer and more near.
Urge the dromedary's speed;
Spur to death the reeling steed;
If perchance ye yet may gain
The mountains that o'erhang the plain.

'Oh thou haughty land of Nod,
Hear the sentence of thy God.
Thou hast said "Of all the hills
Whence, after autumn rains, the rills
    In silver trickle down,
The fairest is that mountain white
Which intercepts the morning light
    From Cain's imperial town.
On its first and gentlest swell
Are pleasant halls where nobles dwell;
And marble porticoes are seen
Peeping through terraced gardens green.
Above are olives, palms, and vines;
And higher yet the dark-blue pines;
And highest on the summit shines
    The crest of everlasting ice.
Here let the God of Abel own
That human art hath wonders shown
    Beyond his boasted paradise."

'Therefore on that proud mountain's crown
    Thy few surviving sons and daughters
Shall see their latest sun go down
    Upon a boundless waste of waters.
None salutes and none replies;
    None heaves a groan or breathes a prayer;
They crouch on earth with tearless eyes,
    And clenched hands, and bristling hair.
The rain pours on: no star illumes
    The blackness of the roaring sky.
And each successive billow booms
    Nigher still and still more nigh.

And now upon the howling blast
The wreaths of spray come thick and fast;
And a great billow by the tempest curled
   Falls with a thundering crash; and all is o'er.
And what is left of all this glorious world?
   A sky without a beam, a sea without a shore.

'Oh thou fair land, where from their starry home
Cherub and seraph oft delight to roam,
Thou city of the thousand towers,
   Thou palace of the golden stairs,
Ye gardens of perennial flowers,
   Ye moated gates, ye breezy squares;
Ye parks amidst whose branches high
Oft peers the squirrel's sparkling eye;
Ye vineyards, in whose trellised shade
Pipes many a youth to many a maid;
Ye ports where rides the gallant ship;
   Ye marts where wealthy burghers meet;
Ye dark green lanes which know the trip
   Of woman's conscious feet;
Ye grassy meads where, when the day is done,
   The shepherd pens his fold;
Ye purple moors on which the setting sun
   Leaves a rich fringe of gold;
Ye wintry deserts where the larches grow;
Ye mountains on whose everlasting snow
   No human foot hath trod;
   Many a fathom shall ye sleep
   Beneath the grey and endless deep,
In the great day of the revenge of God.'

1827

The Country Clergyman's Trip to Cambridge

AN ELECTION BALLAD

As I sat down to breakfast in state,
  At my living of Tithing-cum-Boring,
With Betty beside me to wait,
  Came a rap that almost beat the door in.
I laid down my basin of tea,
  And Betty ceased spreading the toast,
'As sure as a gun, sir,' said she,
  'That must be the knock of the post.'

A letter – and free – bring it here –
  I have no correspondent who franks.
No! yes! Can it be? Why, my dear,
  'Tis our glorious, our Protestant Bankes.
'Dear sir, as I know you desire
  That the Church should receive due protection,
I humbly presume to require
  Your aid at the Cambridge election.

'It has lately been brought to my knowledge,
  That the Ministers fully design
To suppress each cathedral and college,
  And eject every learned divine.
To assist this detestable scheme
  Three nuncios from Rome are come over;
They left Calais on Monday by steam,
  And landed to dinner at Dover.

'An army of grim Cordeliers,
  Well furnished with relics and vermin,
Will follow, Lord Westmoreland fears,
  To effect what their chiefs may determine.
Lollard's bower, good authorities say,
  Is again fitting up for a prison;
And a wood-merchant told me today
  'Tis a wonder how faggots have risen.

'The finance scheme of Canning contains
 A new Easter-offering tax;
And he means to devote all the gains
 To a bounty on thumb-screws and racks.
Your living, so neat and compact –
 Pray, don't let the news give you pain! –
Is promised, I know for a fact,
 To an olive-faced Padre from Spain.'

I read, and I felt my heart bleed,
 Sore wounded with horror and pity;
So I flew, with all possible speed,
 To our Protestant champion's committee.
True gentlemen, kind and well-bred!
 No fleering! no distance! no scorn!
They asked after my wife who is dead,
 And my children who never were born.

They then, like high-principled Tories,
 Called our Sovereign unjust and unsteady,
And assailed him with scandalous stories,
 Till the coach for the voters was ready.
That coach might be well called a casket
 Of learning and brotherly love:
There were parsons in boot and in basket;
 There were parsons below and above.

There were Sneaker and Griper, a pair
 Who stick to Lord Mulesby like leeches;
A smug chaplain of plausible air,
 Who writes my Lord Goslingham's speeches.
Dr Buzz, who alone is a host,
 Who, with arguments weighty as lead,
Proves six times a week in the Post
 That flesh somehow differs from bread.

Dr Nimrod, whose orthodox toes
 Are seldom withdrawn from the stirrup;
Dr Humdrum, whose eloquence flows,
 Like droppings of sweet poppy syrup;
Dr Rosygill puffing and fanning,
 And wiping away perspiration;

Dr Humbug, who proved Mr Canning
   The beast in St John's Revelation.

A layman can scarce form a notion
   Of our wonderful talk on the road;
Of the learning, the wit, and devotion,
   Which almost each syllable showed:
Why divided allegiance agrees
   So ill with our free constitution;
How Catholics swear as they please,
   In hope of the priest's absolution;

How the Bishop of Norwich had bartered
   His faith for a legate's commission;
How Lyndhurst, afraid to be martyr'd,
   Had stooped to a base coalition;
How Papists are cased from compassion
   By bigotry, stronger than steel;
How burning would soon come in fashion,
   And how very bad it must feel.

We were all so much touched and excited
   By a subject so direly sublime,
That the rules of politeness were slighted,
   And we all of us talked at a time;
And in tones, which each moment grew louder,
   Told how we should dress for the show,
And where we should fasten the powder,
   And if we should bellow or no.

Thus from subject to subject we ran,
   And the journey passed pleasantly o'er,
Till at last Dr Humdrum began;
   From that time I remember no more.
At Ware he commenced his prelection,
   In the dullest of clerical drones;
And when next I regained recollection
   We were rumbling o'er Trumpington stones.

1827

Song

O stay, Madonna! stay;
　　'Tis not the dawn of day
That marks the skies with yonder opal streak:
　　The stars in silence shine;
　　Then press thy lips to mine,
And rest upon my neck thy fervid cheek.

O sleep, Madonna! sleep;
　　Leave me to watch and weep
O'er the sad memory of departed joys,
　　O'er hope's extinguished beam,
　　O'er fancy's vanished dream,
O'er all that nature gives and man destroys.

O wake, Madonna! wake;
　　Even now the purple lake
Is dappled o'er with amber flakes of light;
　　A glow is on the hill;
　　And every trickling rill
In golden threads leaps down from yonder height.

O fly, Madonna! fly,
　　Lest day and envy spy
What only love and night may safely know:
　　Fly, and tread softly, dear!
　　Lest those who hate us hear
The sounds of thy light footsteps as they go.

1827

The Deliverance of Vienna

TRANSLATED FROM VINCENZIO DA FILICAIA

'Le corde d'oro elette,' &c.

The chords, the sacred chords of gold,
Strike, oh Muse, in measure bold;
And frame a sparkling wreath of joyous songs
For that great God to whom revenge belongs.
Who shall resist his might,
Who marshals for the fight
Earthquake and thunder, hurricane and flame?
He smote the haughty race
Of unbelieving Thrace,
And turned their rage to fear, their pride to shame.
He looked in wrath from high,
Upon their vast array;
And, in the twinkling of an eye,
Tambour, and trump, and battle-cry,
And steeds, and turbaned infantry,
Passed like a dream away.
Such power defends the mansions of the just:
But, like a city without walls,
The grandeur of the mortal falls
Who glories in his strength, and makes not God his trust.

The proud blasphemers thought all earth their own;
They deemed that soon the whirlwind of their ire
Would sweep down tower and palace, dome and spire,
The Christian altars and the Augustan throne.
And soon, they cried, shall Austria bow
To the dust her lofty brow.
The princedoms of Almayne
Shall wear the Phrygian chain;
In humbler waves shall vassal Tiber roll;

And Rome, a slave forlorn,
Her laurelled tresses shorn,
Shall feel our iron in her inmost soul.
Who shall bid the torrent stay?
Who shall bar the lightning's way?
Who arrest the advancing van
Of the fiery Ottoman?

As the curling smoke wreaths fly
When fresh breezes clear the sky,
Passed away each swelling boast
Of the misbelieving host.
From the Hebrus rolling far
Came the murky cloud of war,
And in shower and tempest dread
Burst on Austria's fenceless head.
But not for vaunt or threat
Didst Thou, oh Lord, forget
The flock so dearly bought, and loved so well.
Even in the very hour
Of guilty pride and power
Full on the circumcised Thy vengeance fell.
Then the fields were heaped with dead,
Then the streams with gore were red,
And every bird of prey, and every beast,
From wood and cavern thronged to Thy great feast.

What terror seized the fiends obscene of Nile!
How wildly, in his place of doom beneath,
Arabia's lying prophet gnashed his teeth,
And cursed his blighted hopes and wasted guile!
When, at the bidding of Thy sovereign might,
Flew on their destined path
Thy messengers of wrath,
Riding on storms and wrapped in deepest night.
The Phthian mountains saw,
And quaked with mystic awe:
The proud Sultana of the Straits bowed down
Her jewelled neck and her embattled crown.
The miscreants, as they raised their eyes

Glaring defiance on Thy skies,
Saw adverse winds and clouds display
The terrors of their black array; —
Saw each portentous star
Whose fiery aspect turned of yore to flight
The iron chariots of the Canaanite
Gird its bright harness for a deadlier war.

Beneath Thy withering look
Their limbs with palsy shook;
Scattered on earth the crescent banners lay;
Trembled with panic fear
Sabre and targe and spear,
Through the proud armies of the rising day.
Faint was each heart, unnerved each hand;
And, if they strove to charge or stand,
Their efforts were as vain
As his who, scared in feverish sleep
By evil dreams, essays to leap,
Then backward falls again.
With a crash of wild dismay,
Their ten thousand ranks gave way;
Fast they broke, and fast they fled;
Trampled, mangled, dying, dead,
Horse and horseman mingled lay;
Till the mountains of the slain
Raised the valleys to the plain.
Be all the glory of Thy name divine!
The swords were ours; the arm, O Lord, was Thine.

Therefore to Thee, beneath whose footstool wait
The powers which erring man calls Chance and Fate,
To Thee who hast laid low
The pride of Europe's foe,
And taught Byzantium's sullen lords to fear,
I pour my spirit out
In a triumphant shout,
And call all ages and all lands to hear.
Thou who evermore endurest,
Loftiest, mightiest, wisest, purest,

Thou whose will destroys or saves,
Dread of tyrants, hope of slaves,
The wreath of glory is from Thee,
And the red sword of victory.
There where exulting Danube's flood
Runs stained with Islam's noblest blood
　　From that tremendous field,
There where in mosque the tyrants met,
And from the crier's minaret
　　Unholy summons pealed,
Pure shrines and temples now shall be
Decked for a worship worthy Thee.
To Thee thy whole creation pays
With mystic sympathy its praise,
　　The air, the earth, the seas:
The day shines forth with livelier beam;
There is a smile upon the stream,
　　An anthem on the breeze.
Glory, they cry, to Him whose might
Hath turned the barbarous foe to flight,
Whose arm protects with power-divine
The city of his favoured line.
The caves, the woods, the rocks, repeat the sound;
The everlasting hills roll the long echoes round.

But, if Thy rescued church may dare
Still to besiege Thy throne with prayer,
Sheathe not, we implore Thee, Lord,
Sheathe not Thy victorious sword.
Still Panonia pines away,
Vassal of a double sway:
Still Thy servants groan in chains,
Still the race which hates Thee reigns:
Part the living from the dead:
Join the members to the head:
Snatch Thine own sheep from yon fell monster's hold;
Let one kind shepherd rule one undivided fold.

He is the victor, only he
Who reaps the fruits of victory.

We conquered once in vain,
When foamed the Ionian waves with gore,
And heaped Lepanto's stormy shore
   With wrecks and Moslem slain.
Yet wretched Cyprus never broke
The Syrian tyrant's iron yoke.
   Shall the twice vanquished foe
   Again repeat his blow?
Shall Europe's sword be hung to rust in peace?
   No – let the red-cross ranks
   Of the triumphant Franks
Bear swift deliverance to the shrines of Greece,
And in her inmost heart let Asia feel
The avenging plagues of Western fire and steel.

   Oh God! for one short moment raise
   The veil which hides those glorious days.
   The flying foes I see Thee urge
   Even to the river's headlong verge.
   Close on their rear the loud uproar
   Of fierce pursuit from Ister's shore
    Comes pealing on the wind;
   The Rab's wild waters are before,
    The Christian sword behind.
   Sons of perdition, speed your flight.
    No earthly spear is in the rest;
   No earthly champion leads to fight
    The warriors of the West.
The Lord of Hosts asserts His old renown,
Scatters, and smites, and slays, and tramples down
Fast, fast, beyond what mortal tongue can say
   Or mortal fancy dream,
He rushes on his prey:
   Till, with the terrors of the wondrous theme
Bewildered and appalled, I cease to sing,
And close my dazzled eye, and rest my wearied wing.

Published in the *Winter's Wreath*, Liverpool, 1828

The Armada

A FRAGMENT

Attend, all ye who list to hear our noble England's praise;
I tell of the thrice famous deeds she wrought in ancient days,
When that great fleet invincible against her bore in vain
The richest spoils of Mexico, the stoutest hearts of Spain.

It was about the lovely close of a warm summer day,
There came a gallant merchant-ship full sail to Plymouth Bay;
Her crew hath seen Castile's black fleet, beyond Aurigny's isle,
At earliest twilight, on the waves lie heaving many a mile.
At sunrise she escaped their van, by God's especial grace;
And the tall Pinta, till the noon, had held her close in chase.
Forthwith a guard at every gun was placed along the wall;
The beacon blazed upon the roof of Edgecumbe's lofty hall;
Many a light fishing-bark put out to pry along the coast,
And with loose rein and bloody spur rode inland many a post.
With his white hair unbonneted, the stout old sheriff comes;
Behind him march the halberdiers; before him sound the
    drums;
His yeomen round the market cross make clear an ample space;
For there behoves him to set up the standard of Her Grace.
And haughtily the trumpets peal, and gaily dance the bells,
As slow upon the labouring wind the royal blazon swells.
Look how the Lion of the sea lifts up his ancient crown,
And underneath his deadly paw treads the gay lilies down.
So stalked he when he turned to flight, on that famed Picard
    field,
Bohemia's plume, and Genoa's bow, and Cæsar's eagle shield.
So glared he when at Agincourt in wrath he turned to bay,
And crushed and torn beneath his claws the princely hunters
    lay.
Ho! strike the flagstaff, sir Knight: ho! scatter flowers, fair
    maids:
Ho! gunners, fire a loud salute: ho! gallants, draw your blades:

Thou sun, shine on her joyously; ye breezes, waft her wide;
Our glorious SEMPER EADEM, the banner of our pride.

   The freshening breeze of eve unfurled that banner's massy
     fold;
The parting gleam of sunshine kissed that haughty scroll of
     gold;
Night sank upon the dusky beach, and on the purple sea,
Such night in England ne'er had been, nor ne'er again shall be.
From Eddystone to Berwick bounds, from Lynn to Milford Bay,
That time of slumber was as bright and busy as the day;
For swift to east and swift to west the ghastly war-flame spread,
High on St Michael's Mount it shone: it shone on Beachy Head.
Far on the deep the Spaniard saw, along each southern shire,
Cape beyond cape; in endless range, those twinkling points of
     fire.
The fisher left his skiff to rock on Tamar's glittering waves:
The rugged miners poured to war from Mendip's sunless caves:
O'er Longleat's towers, o'er Cranbourne's oaks, the fiery herald
     flew:
He roused the shepherds of Stonehenge, the rangers of
     Beaulieu.
Right sharp and quick the bells all night rang out from Bristol
     town,
And ere the day three hundred horse had met on Clifton down;
The sentinel on Whitehall gate looked forth into the night,
And saw o'erhanging Richmond Hill the streak of blood-red
     light.
Then bugle's note and cannon's roar the deathlike silence
     broke,
And with one start, and with one cry, the royal city woke.
At once on all her stately gates arose the answering fires;
At once the wild alarum clashed from all her reeling spires;
From all the batteries of the Tower pealed loud the voice of fear;
And all the thousand masts of Thames sent back a louder cheer:
And from the furthest wards was heard the rush of hurrying
     feet,
And the broad streams of pikes and flags rushed down each
     roaring street;
And broader still became the blaze, and louder still the din,

As fast from every village round the horse came spurring in:
And eastward straight from wild Blackheath the warlike errand
     went,
And roused in many an ancient hall the gallant squires of Kent.
Southward from Surrey's pleasant hills flew those bright
     couriers forth;
High on bleak Hampstead's swarthy moor they started for the
     north;
And on, and on, without a pause, untired they bounded still:
All night from tower to tower they sprang; they sprang from hill
     to hill:
Till the proud peak unfurled the flag o'er Darwin's rocky dales,
Till like volcanoes flared to heaven the stormy hills of Wales,
Till twelve fair counties saw the blaze on Malvern's lonely
     height,
Till streamed in crimson on the wind the Wrekin's crest of light,
Till broad and fierce the star came forth on Ely's stately fane,
And tower and hamlet rose in arms o'er all the boundless plain;
Till Belvoir's lordly terraces the sign to Lincoln sent,
And Lincoln sped the message on o'er the wide vale of Trent;
Till Skiddaw saw the fire that burned on Gaunt's embattled pile,
And the red glare on Skiddaw roused the burghers of Carlisle.

                                                    1832

To William Cavendish Bentinck

INSCRIPTION ON THE STATUE OF
LORD WILLIAM BENTINCK AT CALCUTTA

Who, during seven years, ruled India with eminent
Prudence, Integrity, and Benevolence:
Who, placed at the head of a great Empire, never laid aside
The simplicity and moderation of a private citizen:
Who infused into Oriental despotism the spirit
of British Freedom:
Who never forgot that the end of Government is
The happiness of the Governed:
Who abolished cruel rites:
Who effaced humiliating distinctions:
Who gave liberty to the expression of public opinion:
Whose constant study it was, to elevate the intellectual
And moral character of the Nations committed to his charge:
This Monument
Was erected by men,
Who, differing in Race, in Manners, in Language,
And in Religion,
Cherish, with equal veneration and gratitude,
The memory of his wise, upright,
And paternal Administration.

1835

Epitaph on
Sir Benjamin Heath Malkin
at Calcutta

This monument
Is sacred to the memory
of
Sir Benjamin Heath Malkin, Knight,
One of the Judges of The Supreme Court of Judicature:
A man eminently distinguished
By his literary and scientific attainments,
By his professional learning and ability,
By the clearness and accuracy of his intellect,
By diligence, by patience, by firmness, by love of truth.
By public spirit, ardent and disinterested,
Yet always under the guidance of discretion,
By rigid uprightness, by unostentatious piety,
By the serenity of his temper,
And by the benevolence of his heart.

1837

Benjamin Heath Malkin, born on the 29th September 1797,
died on the 21st October 1837

The Last Buccaneer

The winds were yelling, the waves were swelling,
   The sky was black and drear,
When the crew with eyes of flame brought the ship
     without a name
   Alongside the last Buccaneer.

'Whence flies your sloop full sail before so fierce a gale,
   When all others drive bare on the seas?
Say, come ye from the shore of the holy Salvador,
   Or the gulf of the rich Caribbees?'

'From a shore no search hath found, from a gulf no line
   can sound,
   Without rudder or needle we steer;
Above, below, our bark, dies the sea fowl and the shark,
   As we fly by the last Buccaneer.

'Tonight there shall be heard on the rocks of Cape de
     Verde
   A loud crash, and a louder roar;
And tomorrow shall the deep, with a heavy moaning,
     sweep
   The corpses and wreck to the shore.'

The stately ship of Clyde securely now may ride
   In the breath of the citron shades;
And Severn's towering mast securely now flies fast,
   Through the sea of the balmy Trades.

From St Jago's wealthy port, from Havannah's royal fort,
   The seaman goes forth without fear;
For since that stormy night not a mortal hath had sight
   Of the flag of the last Buccaneer.

                        1839

Epitaph on a Jacobite

To my true king I offered free from stain
Courage and faith; vain faith, and courage vain.
For him, I threw lands, honours, wealth, away,
And one dear hope, that was more prized than they.
For him I languished in a foreign clime,
Grey-haired with sorrow in my manhood's prime;
Heard on Lavernia Scargill's whispering trees,
And pined by Arno for my lovelier Tees;
Beheld each night my home in fevered sleep,
Each morning started from the dream to weep;
Till God, who saw me tried too sorely, gave
The resting place I asked, an early grave.
Oh thou, whom chance leads to this nameless stone,
From that proud country which was once mine own,
By those white cliffs I never more must see,
By that dear language which I spake like thee,
Forget all feuds, and shed one English tear
O'er English dust. A broken heart lies here.

1845

Valentine
to the Hon. Mary C. Stanhope,
daughter of Lord and Lady Mahon

Hail, day of Music, day of Love,
On earth below, in air above.
In air the turtle fondly moans,
The linnet pipes in joyous tones;
On earth the postman toils along,
Bent double by huge bales of song,
Where, rich with many a gorgeous dye,
Blazes all Cupid's heraldry –
Myrtles and roses, doves and sparrows,
Love-knots and altars, lamps and arrows.
What nymph without wild hopes and fears
The double rap this morning hears?
Unnumbered lasses, young and fair,
From Bethnal Green to Belgrave Square,
With cheeks high flushed, and hearts loud beating,
Await the tender annual greeting.
The loveliest lass of all is mine –
Good morrow to my Valentine!

Good morrow, gentle Child! and then
Again good morrow, and again,
Good morrow following still good morrow,
Without one cloud of strife or sorrow.
And when the God to whom we pay
In jest our homages today
Shall come to claim, no more in jest,
His rightful empire o'er thy breast,
Benignant may his aspect be,
His yoke the truest liberty:
And if a tear his power confess,
Be it a tear of happiness.
It shall be so. The Muse displays

The future to her votary's gaze;
Prophetic rage my bosom swells –
I taste the cake – I hear the bells!
From Conduit Street the close array
Of chariots barricades the way
To where I see, with outstretched hand,
Majestic, thy great kinsman stand,*
And half unbend his brow of pride,
As welcoming so fair a bride.
Gay favours, thick as flakes of snow,
Brighten St George's portico:
Within I see the chancel's pale,
The orange flowers, the Brussels veil,
The page on which those fingers white,
Still trembling from the awful rite,
For the last time shall faintly trace
The name of Stanhope's noble race.
I see kind faces round thee pressing,
I hear kind voices whisper blessing;
And with those voices mingles mine –
All good attend my Valentine!

St Valentine's Day, 1851

* The statue of Mr Pitt in Hanover Square

Lines written on
the Night of the 30th of July, 1847

AT THE CLOSE OF AN UNSUCCESSFUL
CONTEST FOR EDINBURGH

The day of tumult, strife, defeat, was o'er;
  Worn out with toil, and noise, and scorn, and spleen,
I slumbered, and in slumber saw once more
  A room in an old mansion,* long unseen.

That room, methought, was curtained from the light;
  Yet through the curtains shone the moon's cold ray
Full on a cradle, where, in linen white,
  Sleeping life's first soft sleep, an infant lay.

Pale flickered on the hearth the dying flame,
  And all was silent in that ancient hall,
Save when by fits on the low night-wind came
  The murmur of the distant waterfall.

And lo! the fairy queens who rule our birth
  Drew nigh to speak the new born baby's doom:
With noiseless step, which left no trace on earth,
  From gloom they came, and vanished into gloom.

Not deigning on the boy a glance to cast
  Swept careless by the gorgeous Queen of Gain;
More scornful still, the Queen of Fashion passed,
  With mincing gait and sneer of cold disdain.

The Queen of Power tossed high her jewelled head,
  And o'er her shoulder threw a wrathful frown:
The Queen of Pleasure on the pillow shed
  Scarce one stray rose-leaf from her fragrant crown.

* Rothley Temple, Leicestershire

Still Fay in long procession followed Fay;
   And still the little couch remained unblest:
But, when those wayward sprites had passed away,
   Came One, the last, the mightiest, and the best.

Oh glorious lady, with the eyes of light
   And laurels clustering round thy lofty brow,
Who by the cradle's side didst watch that night,
   Warbling a sweet strange music, who wast thou?

'Yes, darling; let them go;' so ran the strain:
   'Yes; let them go, gain, fashion, pleasure, power,
And all the busy elves to whose domain
   Belongs the nether sphere, the fleeting hour,

'Without one envious sigh, one anxious scheme,
   The nether sphere, the fleeting hour resign,
Mine is the world of thought, the world of dream,
   Mine all the past, and all the future mine.

'Fortune, that lays in sport the mighty low,
   Age, that to penance turns the joys of youth,
Shall leave untouched the gifts which I bestow,
   The sense of beauty and the thirst of truth.

'Of the fair brotherhood who share my grace,
   I, from thy natal day, pronounce thee free;
And, if for some I keep a nobler place,
   I keep for none a happier than for thee.

'There are who, while to vulgar eyes they seem
   Of all my bounties largely to partake,
Of me as of some rival's handmaid deem,
   And court me but for gain's, power's, fashion's sake.

'To such, though deep their lore, though wide their fame,
   Shall my great mysteries be all unknown:
But thou, through good and evil, praise and blame,
   Wilt not thou love me for myself alone?

'Yes; thou wilt love me with exceeding love;
   And I will tenfold all that love repay,
Still smiling, though the tender may reprove,
   Still faithful, though the trusted may betray.

'For aye mine emblem was, and aye shall be,
   The ever-during plant whose bough I wear,
Brightest and greenest then, when every tree
   That blossoms in the light of Time is bare.

'In the dark hour of shame, I deigned to stand
   Before the frowning peers at Bacon's side:
On a far shore I smoothed with tender hand,
   Through months of pain, the sleepless bed of Hyde;

'I brought the wise and brave of ancient days
   To cheer the cell where Raleigh pined alone:
I lighted Milton's darkness with the blaze
   Of the bright ranks that guard the eternal throne.

'And even so, my child, it is my pleasure
   That thou not then alone shouldst feel me nigh,
When in domestic bliss and studious leisure,
   Thy weeks uncounted come, uncounted fly;

'Not then alone, when myriads, closely pressed
   Around thy car, the shout of triumph raise;
Nor when, in gilded drawing rooms, thy breast
   Swells at the sweeter sound of woman's praise.

'No: when on restless night dawns cheerless morrow,
   When weary soul and wasting body pine,
Thine am I still, in danger, sickness, sorrow,
   In conflict, obloquy, want, exile, thine;

'Thine, where on mountain waves the snowbirds scream,
   Where more than Thule's winter barbs the breeze,
Where scarce, through lowering clouds, one sickly gleam
   Lights the drear May-day of Antarctic seas;

'Thine, when around thy litter's track all day
    White sandhills shall reflect the blinding glare;
Thine, when, through forests breathing death, thy way
    All night shall wind by many a tiger's lair;

'Thine most, when friends turn pale when traitors fly,
    When, hard beset, thy spirit, justly proud,
For truth, peace, freedom, mercy, dares defy
    A sullen priesthood and a raving crowd.

'Amidst the din of all things fell and vile,
    Hate's yell, and envy's hiss, and folly's bray,
Remember me; and with an unforced smile
    See riches, baubles, flatterers, pass away.

'Yes: they will pass away; nor deem it strange:
    They come and go, as comes and goes the sea:
And let them come and go: thou, through all change,
    Fix thy firm gaze on virtue and on me.'

                                    1847

INDEX OF POEM TITLES

INDEX OF FIRST LINES

The Wordsworth Poetry Library

Works of:

Matthew Arnold

William Blake

The Brontë Sisters

Rupert Brooke

Robert Browning

Elizabeth Barrett Browning

Robert Burns

Lord Byron

Geoffrey Chaucer

G. K. Chesterton

John Clare

Samuel Taylor Coleridge

Emily Dickinson

John Donne

John Dryden

Thomas Hardy

George Herbert

Gerard Manley Hopkins

A. E. Housman

James Joyce

John Keats

Rudyard Kipling

D. H. Lawrence

Henry Wadsworth Longfellow

Macaulay

Andrew Marvell

John Milton

Wilfred Owen

'Banjo' Paterson

Edgar Allen Poe

Alexander Pope

John Wilmot, Earl of Rochester

Christina Rossetti

Sir Walter Scott

William Shakespeare

P. B. Shelley

Edmund Spenser

Algernon Swinburne

Alfred Lord Tennyson

Edward Thomas

Walt Whitman

Oscar Wilde

William Wordsworth

W. B. Yeats

Anthologies & Collections

Restoration and
Eighteenth-Century Verse

Nineteenth-Century Verse

Poetry of the First World War

Love Poems

The Metaphysical Poets

The Wordsworth Book of Sonnets